Sounds in Action

Phonological Awareness
Activities and Assessment

By

Yvette Zgonc, M.Ed., LMHC

Crystal Springs
BOOKS

Published by
Crystal Springs Books · Peterborough, New Hampshire
1-800-321-0401 · www.crystalsprings.com

Printed in the United States of America
08 07 06 05   7 8 9

Published by Crystal Springs Books
75 Jaffrey Road
P.O. Box 500
Peterborough, NH 03458
1-800-321-0401
fax: 1-800-337-9929

U.S. Cataloging-in-Publication Data
   (Library of Congress Standards)

Zgonc, Yvette, 1944–
   Sounds in action : phonological awareness activities
and assessments / by Yvette Zgonc.—1st ed.
[160] p. : Ill.; cm.
Summary: An assessment that measures K–2 students'
phonological awareness skills, specific activities for each
skill, activities to make the connection between
phonological awareness and phonics, a discussion of key
research findings, and further reading.
ISBN 1-884548-32-6
1. Language awareness in children. 2. English language —
Phonetics. 3. Children — Language. 4. Phonics — Study
and teaching.   I. Title.
371.46 /5 —dc21   2000   CIP
00-130396

Editor: Cathy Kingery
Cover and Book Design: Susan Dunholter
Illustrations: Rob Ewing
Publishing Manager: Lorraine Walker

Dedication

    This book is dedicated to the memory of my father, Irv Gerber. Although he has been deceased for over 25 years, his powerful influence to pursue and love the field of teaching continues to be with me today.

Acknowledgments

Special thanks to:

My husband, Frank, who puts up with my navigational challenges and who has steered me in the right direction on real roads and on the road of life like a shining North Star.

My three grown sons, Adam, Todd, and Chad, who for years have been willing to be guinea pigs as I tried out activities with them before I tried them out in classrooms.

My mother and best friend, whose encouragement and belief in my abilities helped me believe that I Can.

My sister and brother, with whom I can still be playful.

Linda Albert, without whose driving force I would not have had the courage to venture out into the consulting world, and who hooked me up with Frances Smith, who in turn hooked me up with Bill Blokker, who introduced me to the world of phonological awareness and to the fabulous process of Literacy First and made invaluable suggestions for this book.

All the Cooperative Discipline, SDE, and Literacy First presenters, who continue to be encouragers and cheerleaders.

The SDE family in Peterborough, New Hampshire, from whom I have never heard a discouraging word; Cathy Kingery, who is my talented editor; and Jim Grant, Irv Richardson, Char Forsten, and Lorraine Walker, all of whose unwavering support convinced me to just Do It!

Table of Contents

Phonological Awareness & Phonics Connection

Parent Connection

No significant learning takes place without a significant relationship.
How do you connect with your students daily?
You probably greet them at the door, tell stories about yourself,
find out about their interests, or laugh with them.
Do you believe the Chinese proverb that says that
"a child's life is like a piece of paper on which
every passerby leaves a mark"?

Overview

Introduction

Four-year-old Kayla squealed with delight as her dad read her Dr. Seuss's fun rhyming story *There's a Wocket in My Pocket*. This dad unknowingly was giving Kayla the gift of one of the most important phonological awareness (PA) skills—rhyme. Over 20 years of research has substantiated the need for children to acquire PA skills to be successful readers.

Although a considerable number of children who enter school are blessed with these abilities, it is clear that at least 20 percent to 25 percent of the children who walk into our kindergarten classrooms lack these extremely critical skills. Fortunately, explicit and engaging PA instruction appears to accelerate reading with children who come through our doors with or without these skills.

In order to assist K–2 teachers, reading specialists, speech pathologists, and special education and Title I teachers in helping children acquire these skills, this book is divided into six sections:

- Clarification of the meaning of PA, phonemic awareness, and phonics
- An assessment tool that can measure where a child is on the PA skills sequence
- Engaging activities that teachers can use for whole-group and small-group instruction in PA related to the assessment
- Practical activities that create a PA/phonics connection
- Sample letters and ideas for parents
- Resources

Let's start this journey by your asking yourself where you think you are on the PA continuum. Which statement below best describes your present understanding of PA?

- ❑ 1. I haven't a clue what it is. (That's why I'm reading this book.)
- ❑ 2. I have heard some of the terminology, but I'm not familiar with it.
- ❑ 3. I have a basic understanding and am implementing some PA strategies in my classroom.
- ❑ 4. I have a good understanding and use it regularly.
- ❑ 5. I can teach it.

My job is not to bore those readers who are well grounded in these concepts (those of you who selected statement 3, 4, or 5) while at the same time refraining from overwhelming those who are just starting out (those of you who selected statement 1 or 2). Please enjoy this journey no matter where you are on the PA continuum. My wish for you is that this book will offer some new ideas to add to your existing repertoire to help your children become fluent readers.

What Is Phonological Awareness?

Phonological awareness (PA) is the understanding that our spoken language is made up of words and that our words are made up of individual units of sound called *phonemes*. Children need to be able to manipulate these sounds in order to become fluent readers. PA skills include concept of spoken word, rhyme, syllables, phonemes, and phoneme manipulation. It's important to note that phonemes represent a skill that fits under PA. Therefore, phonemic awareness also fits beneath PA. However, the terms *phonemic awareness* and *phonological awareness* are often interchanged in the literature.

Joseph Torgesen and Patricia Mathes of Florida State University define PA as one's sensitivity to or explicit awareness of the phonological structure of words in one's language. It involves the ability to notice, think about, and manipulate the individual sounds in words. In addition, Torgesen and Mathes report that PA is important for two reasons: it helps children understand the alphabetic principle and notice the regular ways in which letters represent sounds in words, and it enables the generation of possibilities for words in context that are only partially "sounded out."

It is critical to recognize that PA is an oral skill independent of print, whereas phonics is both a visual (i.e., print) and an oral (i.e., sound) skill. Phonics and PA are inextricably woven together. To distinguish between PA and phonics, try this: when you think of PA, think ears (perhaps thinking of a PA system might help); when you think of phonics, think eyes and ears.

Research indicates that a child's level of PA and phonemic awareness is highly correlated to reading and spelling success. PA by itself, however, is not enough. It needs to be combined with a systematic, explicit phonics program and integrated with a literature- and language-rich environment for all students. This balanced approach to teaching reading gives students the best chance at reading fluently by the end of third grade. Providing struggling readers with intensive PA instruction (15 to 20 minutes a day, for a total of 12 to 14 hours) has been shown to result in considerable gains.

Children can be trained in phonological awareness both before and during the acquisition of reading skills.

Why Is Phonological Awareness So Important?

In her book *Phonemic Awareness: Playing with Sounds to Strengthen Beginning Reading Skills* (see page 158), Jo Fitzpatrick states that children must be able to hear and manipulate oral sound patterns before they can relate them to print. Phonics instruction builds on a child's ability to segment and blend together sounds he/she hears.

In addition, our language is built on the alphabetic principle; that is, letters have names and sounds, and when these sounds are combined, they form words. PA helps children understand the alphabetic principle and enhances their ability to decode. Decoding to the point of automaticity is the first of two critical reading skills. The second is putting words together for meaning and comprehension.

Why Is Phonological Awareness So Difficult?

Why is PA so difficult for some children? Think about how children hear the words we speak. For instance, mom does not say, "Ralphie, come in and feed the /d/ /o/ /g/"; she says, "Feed the dog." She coarticulates, or blends, the sounds. It is therefore difficult for many children to hear the distinct sounds in words. Have you ever listened to two people speaking a language that was totally foreign to you? You probably had difficulty telling how many words they said in each sentence, let alone how many phonemes were in each word.

Key Research Findings

Phonological awareness and *phonemic awareness* seem to be popular buzz-words. What is all the hoopla about? A profound amount of research has been conducted to support the need to teach these skills to students. The convincing research citings below should reinforce the sense of urgency to integrate PA activities into the language arts block.

Remember, PA is the idea that our language is made up of words and that our words are made up of individual units of sound called *phonemes*. Neither PA nor phonemic awareness is the same as phonics. Phonics helps students see the relationship among letters, letter patterns, and sounds. You have probably noticed, however, a PA component to phonics, since sounds are very much involved. *Phonological awareness* is an umbrella term that includes concept of spoken word, rhyme, syllables, phonemes, and phoneme manipulation. Phonemic awareness, on the other hand, deals with the manipulation of the phonemes in words. Although phonemic awareness fits beneath the umbrella term *phonological awareness*, these two terms are consistently interchanged in the literature, as they are in the following research citings.

- Phonemic awareness is the best single predictor of reading ability in kindergarten, followed by knowledge of letter names and kindergarten teacher predictions (Share, Jorm, MacLean, and Matthews 1984).

- Without direct instructional support, phonemic awareness eludes roughly 25 percent of middle-class first-graders and substantially more of those who come from less literacy-rich backgrounds. These children experience serious difficulty in learning to read and write (Adams 1990).

- Phonemic awareness is more highly related to learning to read than tests of general intelligence, reading readiness, and listening comprehension (Stanovich, Cunningham, and Feeman 1984).

- A child's level of phonemic awareness on entering school is widely held to be the strongest single determinant of the success that he or she will experience in learning to read—or, conversely, the likelihood that he or she will fail (Adams 1990; Stanovich 1986).

- Phonemic awareness can be developed through instruction, and, furthermore, doing so significantly accelerates children's subsequent reading and writing achievement (Ball and Blachman 1991; Bynre and Fielding-Barnsley 1991, 1993, 1995).

- Children need solid phonemic awareness training in order for phonics instruction to be effective (Blevins 1997).

- Phonemic awareness is both a prerequisite for and a consequence of learning to read (Adams 1990; Morais 1979; Yopp 1992).

- Phonemic awareness is the first component of effective reading instruction (Moats 1996).

- The predictive nature of phonological awareness has been demonstrated not only among English-speaking students but among those speaking Swedish (Lundberg, Olofsson, and Wall 1980), Spanish (Manrique and Gramigna 1984), French (Alegria, Pignot, and Morais 1982), Italian (Cossu, Shankweiler, Liberman, Tola, and Katz 1988), Portuguese (Cardoso-Martins 1995), and Russian (Elkonin 1973).

- Most children who experience difficulty acquiring early reading skills can be shown to lag behind in the development of phonological awareness (Felton and Wood 1989).

- Children who begin reading instruction with higher levels of phonological awareness end up with better word-reading skills than their peers at the end of first and second grade (Juel, Griffith, and Gough 1986; Stanovich, Cunningham, and Cramer 1984).

- Approximately 80 percent of children learn how to read, regardless of the method we use with them, precisely because they have this natural phonological awareness capacity and sufficient verbal memory to master sound/symbol rules. A significant number of the other 20 percent have average to above-average intelligence and otherwise good oral language skills. What they often lack is phonological awareness (Lenchner 1997).

- Research strongly suggests that children who possess phonological awareness skills are generally better readers and spellers—and that deficits in these skills are strong predictors of reading and spelling disabilities. This remarkable discovery has been documented throughout the world over the past 20 years and has been considered a "scientific success story" (Stanovich 1987).

Tips for Sounding Out Letters

Paramount to teaching PA is the ability to say the sounds of letters correctly. Many teachers who are recent college graduates have told me that learning the sounds of letters was not taught in their college courses, while veteran teachers lament that the sounds were taught, but taught incorrectly. If you have a speech pathologist at your school, then you have a local expert at your disposal. This person, like all speech pathologists, has known about PA for years and will be a great resource to you.

First of all, you'll notice that many of the letters in this book are surrounded by slashes. Whenever you see a letter that has a slash on either side, that means you should say the sound of the letter, not the name of the letter. If you ask a child to tell you the sound of a letter and he/she says the name of the letter instead, ask, "That is the name of the letter; what is the sound?"

Let's start with the sounds of three letters: /b/, /d/, and /g/. Think about the sound that begins the word *boy*. Many of us were taught to say "buh." That is incorrect. Speech pathologists will tell you that you cannot say that sound without a vowel sound after it, but you must de-emphasize the vowel sound, or clip it. It may help to think about how you say the sound that ends the word *club*. The same thing applies when saying the sound that begins the word *dog* and the sound that begins the word *go*. Clip them so you don't add an "uh."

Say the sound that begins the word *boy* while putting the first and second fingers of one hand on your voice box. You will feel a vibration. This is a *voiced*, consonant sound. Do the same for the sound that begins *dog* and the sound that begins *go*. You'll notice that all three are voiced sounds. They are also *stop sounds* because you cannot say the sounds continuously.

Now say the sound that begins the word *pet*. Is that voiced or voiceless? Put two fingers on your voice box when you say the sound. In addition, put your other hand in front of your mouth. You should not feel your vocal cords vibrate, and you should feel and hear air coming out of your mouth. This is a *voiceless*, *plosive* sound. You should not hear a voiced sound. Rather, it is a forceful whisper.

Try saying the sound that begins the word *kitten* and the sound that begins the word *top*. Put two fingers on your voice box and put your other hand in front of your mouth as you say each sound. What did you notice? Are these voiced or voiceless sounds? Indeed, they are voiceless, plosive sounds. You should have felt the air on your hand as you said them.

Another group of sounds that you should know about are *continuant* sounds, so called because you can stretch them. Examples are /m/, /n/, and /s/. When blending sounds, it is easier to blend continuants than stop sounds. Try blending *man*: mmmmmmmaaaaaaannnnnnn. Now try blending *bat*. You cannot stretch the /b/ and /t/. Starting with continuant sounds when introducing the alphabet will help children blend words early in their acquisition of knowledge about letters and sounds.

The 44 Sounds of English

CONSONANT SOUNDS

1. /b/ (bit)
2. /d/ (dog)
3. /f/ (fat)
4. /g/ (game)
5. /h/ (hop)
6. /j/ (jump)
7. /k/ (kite)
8. /l/ (leaf)
9. /m/ (map)
10. /n/ (not)
11. /p/ (put)
12. /r/ (rake)
13. /s/ (sit)
14. /t/ (tap)
15. /v/ (vest)
16. /w/ (window)
17. /y/ (yellow)
18. /z/ (zebra)
19. /ch/ (chip)
20. /sh/ (shop)
21. /zh/ (treasure)
22. /th/ (think)
23. /th̸/ (though)
24. /hw/ (when)
25. /ng/ (king)

VOWEL SOUNDS

26. /ā/ (make)
27. /ē/ (teeth)
28. /ī/ (kite)
29. /o/ (soap)
30. /yo͞o/ (cube)
31. /a/ (dad)
32. /e/ (bet)
33. /i/ (sit)
34. /o/ (cot)
35. /u/ (hut)
36. /ə/ (ahead)
37. /â/ (air)
38. /û/ (bird)
39. /ä/ (far)
40. /ô/ (ball)
41. /oi/ (toy)
42. /ou/ (mouse)
43. /o͞o/ (soon)
44. /o͝o/ (look)

Stop Sounds **(Voiced)**	**b, d, g, j**	
Stop Sounds **(Voiceless)**	**h, k, p, t**	
Continuant **Sounds** **(Voiced)**	**a, e, i, l, m, n, o, r, u, v, w, y, z**	
Continuant **Sounds** **(Voiceless)**	**f, s**	
Letters Taking **On Other Sounds**	**c = /k/ or /s/ can, city** **qu = /k/ /w/ quick** **x = /k/ /s/ fox**	(*q* generally takes on the sound of /k/ and is usually followed by a *u*.)

Phonological Awareness Skills Sequence

PA includes a series of skills, ranging from easy to difficult, that must eventually be acquired. The main components include the following:

Concept of Spoken Word (Sentence Segmentation)

- **The ability to distinguish words in a sentence**

  Example: I like apples. (three words)

Rhyme

- **The ability to recognize rhyme, complete rhyme, and produce rhyme**

  Example: Does *pick* rhyme with *stick*?

  Example: Complete this rhyme: Humpty Dumpty sat on a wall. Humpty Dumpty had a great _____.

  Example: What word or pretend word rhymes with *ball*?

Syllables

- **The ability to blend, segment, and delete syllables**

  Example: Foot–ball together says *football*.

  Example: Clap the word parts in *rainbow*. (two claps)

  Example: Say *outside* without *side*. (out)

Phonemes

- **The ability to recognize initial and final sounds in words**

  Example: What is the first sound in the word *dot*? /d/

  Example: What is the last sound in the word *sun*? /n/

- **The ability to blend onset and rime**

  Example: What is this word? /t/ /op/ (top)

- **The ability to blend, segment, and delete phonemes**

  Example: /p/ /i/ /g/. What's the word? (pig)

  Example: What are the individual sounds that you hear in *pot*? /p/ /o/ /t/

  Example: Say *take* without /t/. (ake)

  Example: Say *big* without /g/. (bi)

Phoneme Manipulation

• **The ability to add and/or substitute phonemes**

Example: Say /it/. Now add /s/. (sit)

Example: Replace the first sound in *back* with /t/. (tack)

Example: Replace the last sound in *bug* with /n/. (bun)

Thoughts to Ponder

Think about what you just read. What is your present understanding of PA? If someone asked you to define PA at this time, what would you say?

_____

_____

_____

_____

_____

Tips on Tricky Phonemes

Consonant blends keep their own names.

blue   /b/ /l/ /u/

stop   /s/ /t/ /o/ /p/

R-controlled is one sound.

horse   /h/ /or/ /s/

bird   /b/ /ir/ /d/

Diphthongs are one sound.

boy   /b/ /oy/

mouse   /m/ /ou/ /s/

The letters *ng* represent one sound.

king   /k/ /i/ /ng/

sang   /s/ /a/ /ng/

Digraphs are one sound.

ship   /sh/ /i/ /p/

them   /th/ /e/ /m/

The letter *x* represents two sounds.

box   /b/ /o/ /k/ /s/

six   /s/ /i/ /k/ /s/

How many phonemes in these tricky words?

1. church _____   6. though _____

2. ring   _____   7. found   _____

3. three   _____   8. precious _____

4. window _____   9. Florida _____

5. table   _____   10. fix   _____

Answers:

1. /ch/ /ur/ /ch/
2. /r/ /i/ /ng/
3. /th/ /r/ /e/
4. /w/ /i/ /n/ /d/ /ow/
5. /t/ /a/ /b/ /l/
6. /th/ /o/
7. /f/ /ou/ /n/ /d/
8. /p/ /r/ /e/ /sh/ /u/ /s/
9. /F/ /l/ /or/ /i/ /d/ /a/
10. /f/ /i/ /k/ /s/

You can have phonological awareness without phonics, but
you can't have phonics without phonological awareness.
When you think of phonological awareness,
think ears. It is independent of print. When you think of phonics,
think eyes and ears.

One of the ways in which the brain attends to and retains information is through frequent feedback. Learner-controlled feedback is even more powerful than teacher feedback. The following question and answers offer you quick, learner-controlled feedback. The four Brain Check sections in this book give you several opportunities to experience this if you choose to.

What is phonological awareness? Choose from the following answers. To find out if you are correct, see the explanations on the following pages.

A. Phonological awareness is the study of the structure of our language, and its optimal training is through whole-group instruction.

B. Phonological awareness is a language development skill that must accompany print.

C. Phonological awareness is an understanding of the different ways in which our spoken language can be broken down and manipulated.

You chose A: Phonological awareness is the study of the structure of the words that make up our language, and its optimal training is through whole-group instruction.

It's true that PA is the study of the structure of our language, but what makes this statement false is the clause *its optimal training is through whole-group instruction.*

Children enter your classroom at different places on the PA skills sequence. You might have little Randy come in not knowing that the sentence "I like you" consists of three different words. Meanwhile, little Kayla comes in not only knowing that, but she can write the sentence with all the words spelled correctly. After you assess these students, the most effective intervention would be to work with Randy in a small group or individually.

However, whole-class instruction is still very important. It is recommended that kindergarten and first-grade teachers teach PA 15 minutes a day to the entire class and an additional 15 minutes to those students experiencing difficulty. Second-grade teachers should teach PA to the whole class for five to 10 minutes and for an additional 15 minutes in small groups to struggling readers.

Try again. You're very close. Go back and select another alternative to the answer to the question "What is phonological awareness?"

You chose B: Phonological awareness is a language development skill that must accompany print.

Actually, you may have overlooked the trick to remembering the difference between PA and phonics. What makes this statement false are the words *must accompany print.* Remember, when you think of PA, think ears. When you think of phonics, think eyes and ears. Phonics includes letter-sound correspondence and involves print. PA is an oral skill where students need to be aware of the sounds in our words and must learn to manipulate those sounds.

I know you can do it. Go back and select another answer.

You chose C: Good thinking! That is the correct answer. Phonological awareness is an understanding of the different ways in which our spoken language can be broken down and manipulated.

Here is another piece of information on PA that you might find useful: the terms *phonological awareness* and *phonemic awareness* are often interchanged in the literature, but they are different. PA includes all the skills in the PA skills sequence, including concept of spoken word (sentence segmentation), rhyme, syllables, and phonemes, as well as phoneme manipulation. Phonemic awareness is more specific and includes only the awareness and manipulation of phonemes, or individual sounds in words (including blending, segmenting, and deleting), and manipulation of sounds. Phonemic awareness fits underneath the umbrella of PA. (Turn to the phonological awareness skills sequence on page 20 and notice where phonemes fit.)

Neither PA nor phonemic awareness is the same as phonics. Phonics helps students see the relationship among letters, letter patterns, and sounds. However, you have probably noticed a PA component to phonics, since sounds are very much involved.

The focus of the next section of this book, the Phonological Awareness Skills Test, will help you determine if and where your students lack PA skills.

Purkey, Zimmerman, and Allebrand have said
that reading and self-concept are so interwoven
that students who view themselves as poor readers also view
themselves as having little personal worth. Do you agree?

Assessment

Phonological Awareness Skills Test

The Phonological Awareness Skills Test (PAST) in this book is an informal, diagnostic, individually administered assessment tool to help you determine the point of instruction for your students and monitor progress made from doing the activities you select. Because it is not a normed test, there can be flexibility in its administration. For example, you can reteach the directions as necessary or add your own word for the child to blend, segment, or delete if you want to gather additional information on a particular student.

The materials the administrator of the assessment needs include the assessment itself, a pencil, and counters or chips for the student to use for the segmentation part. If counters are not available, the student can clap the number of segments instead. The assessment is administered orally since PA has to do with the sounds of language.

When Skills Are Typically Mastered

Although children develop their PA skills at different rates, it is helpful to have a general window of when specific skills are typically mastered. The following is a suggested timeline.

Skill	Typically mastered
Concept of spoken word (sentence segmentation)	Preschool
Rhyme recognition	Preschool
Rhyme completion	Preschool/kindergarten
Rhyme production	Kindergarten
Syllable blending	Preschool/kindergarten
Syllable segmentation	Kindergarten
Syllable deletion	Kindergarten
Phoneme isolation of initial sound	Kindergarten
Phoneme isolation of final sound	Kindergarten/first grade
Phoneme blending (onset and rime)	First grade
Phoneme blending (all phonemes)	First grade
Phoneme segmentation	First grade
Phoneme deletion of initial sound	First grade
Phoneme deletion of final sound	First grade
Phoneme deletion of first sound in consonant blend	Second grade
Phoneme substitution	Second grade (some first)

Note: In order to make the test user-friendly and time-efficient, the skills of rhyme completion and phoneme blending of onset and rime are not measured. However, since the skills are sequential, if a student masters rhyme production, he/she should also be able to do rhyme completion. By the same token, if a student masters phoneme blending, he/she should also be able to master blending of onset and rime.

Questions and Answers
How to Get the Most out of the Assessment

QUESTION

At what age do students typically master the specific PA skills on the assessment?

ANSWER

Generally, preschoolers are able to master isolation of spoken word, rhyme recognition (some can do rhyme completion), and syllable blending. Kindergartners can master those skills plus rhyme completion, rhyme production, syllable segmentation, syllable deletion, and isolation of the initial sound of a word. Many can master isolation of final sounds as well. First-graders can master the above skills plus phoneme blending, phoneme segmentation, and deletion of initial and final sounds of words. Some can do phoneme substitution. Second-graders can master the above skills, along with phoneme deletion of the first sound in a consonant blend and phoneme substitution.

QUESTION

How fast do you say the sentences in the sentence segmentation section?

ANSWER

Talk in a normal conversational speed. If you tend to speak rapidly, slow it down, but speak in a natural, conversational voice.

QUESTION

Do you administer the entire test to every child?

ANSWER

"Best practices" suggests that you should assess every student. However, for those students who do not appear to be struggling, you may not want to administer any of it. Be aware, though, that sometimes a student only *appears* to be doing OK. Such a child may have a good sight-word vocabulary because early words in books are almost always in a student's oral vocabulary. But once students reach the latter part of third grade, they begin to encounter many words not in their oral vocabulary, and some students then have difficulty decoding these words due to a lack of PA skills.

Also, consider the grade level of the child when administering portions of the test. You may not want to give sentence segmentation to a second-grader because it is too easy. On the other hand, some of the latter part of the assessment would go past the frustration level of most kindergarten children. Administer the test until the child reaches a frustration level; typically, if he/she misses three out of six, stop. However, use your judgment. Some children get stuck on rhyme but can do syllable blending without any problem.

Start at the section where they will have a success rate of at least five out of six correct, and go from there. You can use your judgment, based on kid-watching and other school assessments, to make your decision about where to begin administering the test. However, if you are unsure, start at the beginning (concept of spoken word). Erring on the side of "too easy" when choosing where to begin the assessment is a good rule of thumb.

QUESTION

How many questions should a child master on each section of the assessment to be successful?

ANSWER

To be successful, they need to master at least five out of six, but compare the grade level of the child with the grade level at which a skill is typically mastered.

QUESTION

What do you do with the information you get from giving the test?

ANSWER

Look at the first section where the child missed two or more answers and use the activities in this book that relate to that section. You can do those activities with the whole class, with a small group, or individually.

QUESTION

How long does it take to administer the test?

ANSWER

That depends on how much of the test you administer to the student. Typically, it takes 10 to 15 minutes. It can be administered in two separate sittings.

QUESTION

How do I find the time to give this test to my students?

ANSWER

There are several options. Consider having an instructional aide or volunteer work with the rest of the class while you test. Some teachers assess during sustained silent reading, while others do it while students are in flex groups or centers.

QUESTION

When and how often should this assessment be administered?

ANSWER

Consider assessing two to three times a year. The first test, or pretest, can be given in August or September. Some kindergarten teachers prefer to wait until January to give a PA assessment due to the diversity of children's home-language environments. After students experience PA instruction and activities for the first part of the year in kindergarten, it may be easier to tell who is not progressing and therefore requires intervention. Other kindergarten teachers like to get baseline data on their students and prefer to give the pretest in August.

Regardless, after the children experience whole-group and/or small-group activities relating to the assessment, it should be given in January to monitor progress. A final test, or post-test, should be given in April or May. Some teachers copy the tests on different-colored paper to help identify when the assessment was given—for instance, yellow in August, red in December, and green in April.

It is not necessary to repeat the section(s) of the test where the child scored at least five out of six correct. Each time the assessment is given again, start at the point where the child made more than one error out of six questions.

Phonological Awareness Skills Test (PAST)

Name _____   Date _____

Teacher _____   Grade _____

Concept of Spoken Word

Tell the student you are going to play a game with words and colored chips. Use the sentence "Joey likes cake" as an example. As you say each word of the sentence, push a colored chip forward—one chip per word. Then ask the child to do it. Once he/she understands the skill, read each sentence to the student and ask him/her to repeat the sentence while pushing up one chip for each word. Put a check in the box to the right of the sentence if the child does it correctly.

1. Tom ran home. (3) ☐

2. I have two pets. (4) ☐

3. Did you eat lunch? (4) ☐

4. What are you doing? (4) ☐

5. Terry loves to play soccer. (5) ☐

6. Yesterday it rained. (3) ☐

Total _____

Rhyme Recognition

Tell the child that two words that sound alike at the end, such as *hat* and *sat*, are rhyming words. Ask if *sit* and *bit* rhyme. (Yes.) Then ask if *chair* and *boy* rhyme. (No.) If the child appears to grasp the skill, do the same for each of the following pairs of words. Put a check in the box to the right of the pair if the child answers correctly.

1. bed – fed (yes) ☐

2. top – hop (yes) ☐

3. run – soap (no) ☐

4. hand – sand (yes) ☐

5. funny – bunny (yes) ☐

6. girl – giant (no) ☐

Total _____

Rhyme Production

Tell the child that you are going to say a word, and he/she is to tell you a word that rhymes with it. The answer can be a real word or a nonsense word. Ask the child to tell you a word that rhymes with *sit*. Possible answers include *bit, fit, mit, pit, dit,* and *jit*. Put a check in the box to the right if the child answers correctly. Write down the child's answers on the lines provided.

1. pain ☐ _____　　4. see ☐ _____

2. cake ☐ _____　　5. dark ☐ _____

3. hop ☐ _____　　6. candy ☐ _____

Total _____

Syllable Blending

Tell the child you are going to say a word in a funny way. The job of the student is to put the parts together and say the whole word. Give these examples, pausing between syllables: out–side (outside), ro–bot (robot). Have the child say the sample words normally. Then do the following words and put a check in the box to the right if he/she says them correctly.

1. pen - cil　　　　☐
2. rain - bow　　　☐
3. pop - corn　　　☐
4. black - board　☐
5. side - walk　　☐
6. pa - per　　　　☐

Total _____

Syllable Segmentation

Tell the student that you are going to say a word and then break it into parts, or syllables. First say *rainbow* normally. Clap out the two parts in *rainbow* while saying each part. Then push up a chip as you say each syllable. Read each of the following words and ask the child to push up a chip while saying each syllable. It is not necessary to clap the syllables again unless the skill needs to be retaught. Put a check in the box to the right if the child does it correctly.

1. sometime (2)　　☐
2. basket (2)　　　☐
3. bedroom (2)　　☐
4. fantastic (3)　　☐
5. maybe (2)　　　☐
6. helicopter (4)　☐

Total _____

— 35 —

Syllable Deletion

Tell the student you are going to play a game with words where one part of the word is left out. For example, *sunshine* without *shine* is *sun*. Ask the student to say *airline* without *air*. He/she should say *line*. Using the words below, tell the child the syllable to leave off. Use this sentence structure: "Say (down)town without *down*." Put a check in the box to the right if the student deletes the correct syllable.

1. (down)town   town   □
2. (in)side   side   □
3. for(get)   for   □
4. bas(ket)   bas   □
5. af(ter)   af   □
6. (skate)board   board   □

Total _____

Phoneme Isolation of Initial Sounds

Tell the child you are going to say a word, and he/she is to tell you the first sound of that word. Ask the child what the first sound is in the word *top*. The child should say /t/. Do the same with the words below and put a check in the box to the right if the child says the first sound correctly.

1. big   /b/   □
2. land   /l/   □
3. farm   /f/   □
4. apple   /a/   □
5. desk   /d/   □
6. ship   /sh/   □

Total _____

Phoneme Isolation of Final Sounds

Tell the child you are going to say a word, and he/she is to tell you the last sound in the word. Ask the child what the last sound is in the word *pot*. The child should say /t/. Do the same with the words below and put a check in the box to the right if the child says the sound correctly.

1. pick   /k/   □
2. ran   /n/   □
3. fill   /l/   □
4. bug   /g/   □
5. same   /m/   □
6. tooth   /th/   □

Total _____

Phoneme Blending

Tell the student that you are going to separate all the sounds in a word, and he/she is to say the whole word. Do these examples by segmenting each sound and having the student say the whole word; for example, /s/ /i/ /t/ is *sit*, and /s/ /t/ /o/ /p/ is *stop*. Read each word in segmented fashion. Put a check in the box to the right if the student says the whole word correctly.

1. /m/ /e/   me   ☐
2. /b/ /e/ /d/   bed   ☐
3. /h/ /a/ /t/   hat   ☐
4. /m/ /u/ /s/ /t/   must   ☐
5. /sh/ /o/ /p/   shop   ☐
6. /p/ /l/ /a/ /n/ /t/   plant   ☐

Total _____

Phoneme Segmentation

Tell the student that you're going to play a game with all the sounds in the words below. As an example, show the student the three sounds in *dime*. Push up a chip for each sound you say—/d/ /i/ /m/. Ask the student to try it with the word *hat*. Read each of the following words and ask him/her to push up a chip for each sound. Put a check in the box to the right if he/she does it correctly.

1. in (2)   ☐
2. at (2)   ☐
3. name (3)   ☐
4. ship (3)   ☐
5. sock (3)   ☐
6. chin (3)   ☐

Total _____

Phoneme Deletion of Initial Sounds

Tell the child you will be playing a word game where the beginning sound of a word is left off. For example, *bed* without /b/ is *ed*. Ask the child to say *can* without /c/. The answer is *an*. Read each word below and tell the child the beginning sound to leave off. Put a check in the box to the right if the child does it correctly.

1. (s)un   un   ☐
2. (p)ig   ig   ☐
3. (m)op   op   ☐
4. (n)eck   eck   ☐
5. (b)at   at   ☐
6. (t)ape   ape   ☐

Total _____

Phoneme Deletion of Final Sounds

Tell the child that in this word game, the final sound of a word is left off. For example, *goat* without /t/ is *go*. Ask the child to say *meat* without /t/. The answer is *me*. Read each word and tell the child the ending sound to leave off. Put a check in the box to the right if the child does it correctly.

1. ro/s/e   row   ☐
2. trai/n/   tray   ☐
3. grou/p/   grew   ☐
4. sea/t/   sea   ☐
5. ba/k/e   bay   ☐
6. in/ch/   in   ☐

Total _____

Phoneme Deletion of First Sound in Consonant Blend

Tell the student to make new words by taking the first sound off a consonant blend. Example: The word *crow* without /k/ is *row*. Ask the student to say *still* without /s/. The answer is *till*. Do the following words with the student and put a check in the box to the right if he/she does it correctly.

1. Say *clap* without /k/.   lap   ☐
2. Say *stop* without /s/.   top   ☐
3. Say *trust* without /t/.   rust   ☐
4. Say *black* without /b/.   lack   ☐
5. Say *drip* without /d/.   rip   ☐
6. Say *smile* without /s/.   mile   ☐

Total _____

Phoneme Substitution

Tell the child you will be playing a very different game with sounds of words. You are going to ask him/her to take off the first sound of a word and replace it with another sound. Example: Replace the first sound in *pail* with /m/. The new word is *mail*. Ask the child to replace the first sound in *top* with /h/. The answer is *hop*. Ask the child to do the same with the rest of these words; if he/she answers correctly, put a check in the box on the right.

1. Replace the first sound in *man* with /k/.   can   ☐
2. Replace the first sound in *pig* with /d/.   dig   ☐
3. Replace the first sound in *sack* with /t/.   tack   ☐
4. Replace the first sound in *well* with /f/.   fell   ☐
5. Replace the first sound in *bed* with /r/.   red   ☐
6. Replace the first sound in *shop* with /ch/.   chop   ☐

Total _____

The more ways we teach kids, the more ways we reach kids.
The more pathways in the brain into which we put information,
the more pathways are available from which students can
retrieve information.

PAST Progress Report

Progress report for: _____
student's name

Below each main skill are examples with a box next to each. Based on the PAST, put a check in the box if the child masters five of the six questions on the subtest. The grade levels listed indicate when a skill is typically mastered.

Concept of Spoken Word

✓ **The ability to distinguish oral words in a sentence**

☐ I like apples. (Three words) (Preschool)

Rhyme

✓ **The ability to recognize and produce rhyme**

☐ Does *pick* rhyme with *stick*? (Yes) (Preschool)

☐ What word or pretend word rhymes with *ball*? (fall, tall, dall, etc.) (Kindergarten)

Syllables

✓ **The ability to blend, segment, and delete syllables**

☐ Foot–ball together says *football*. (Preschool to kindergarten)

☐ Clap the word parts in *rainbow*. (Two claps) (Kindergarten)

☐ Say *outside* without *side*. (out) (Kindergarten)

Phonemes

✓ **The ability to recognize initial and final sounds in words**

☐ What is the first sound in the word *dot*? (/d/) (Kindergarten)

☐ What is the last sound in the word *sun*? (/n/) (Kindergarten to first grade)

✓ **The ability to blend, segment, and delete phonemes**

☐ /p/ /i/ /g/ What's the word? (pig) (First grade)

☐ What are the individual sounds you hear in *dot*? (/d/ /o/ /t/) (First grade)

☐ Say *take* without /t/. (ake) (First grade)

☐ Say *bug* without /g/. (bu) (First grade)

☐ Say *stop* without /s/. (top) (Second grade)

Phoneme Manipulation

✓ The ability to substitute phonemes

☐ Replace the first sound in *back* with /t/. (tack) (First to second grade)

CLASS RECORD OF THE PAST

Pretest Date: _____   **Post-Test Date:** _____

Student's Name	Concept of Spoken Word		Rhyme Recognition		Rhyme Production		Syllable Blending		Syllable Segmentation		Syllable Deletion		Isolation of Initial Sounds	

CLASS RECORD OF THE PAST

Pretest Date: _____

Post-Test Date: _____

Student's Name	Isolation of Final Sounds		Phoneme Blending		Phoneme Segmentation		Deletion of Initial Sounds		Deletion of Final Sounds		Deletion of First Sound in Cons. Blend		Phoneme Substitution	

What is the purpose of assessing a student in phonological awareness? Choose one of the following responses.

A. The purpose of assessing a student in phonological awareness is to diagnose the student to determine where he/she is performing on the PA skills sequence. Then the teacher can prescribe interventions, make instructional adjustments, or plan small-group activities for the student.

B. The purpose of assessing a student in phonological awareness is to meet the assessment requirements of the district.

C. The purpose of assessing a student in phonological awareness is because I said that when I became a teacher I couldn't wait to be the one giving the tests instead of the one taking them.

You chose A, and that is absolutely right. The purpose of assessing a student in phonological awareness is to diagnose the student to determine where he/she is performing on the PA skills sequence.

Just as a doctor diagnoses patients and decides on appropriate prescriptions, you are diagnosing your students so that you can choose appropriate interventions or instructional adjustments to assist each student in getting to the next level. Small-group activities concentrating on the skill on which a child needs to work may be appropriate. You then monitor the student to see if your interventions succeeded. If they did not, you re-teach, perhaps through different modalities, and then re-assess.

You chose B: The purpose of assessing a student in phonological awareness is to meet the assessment requirements of the district.

Indeed, meeting the assessment requirements of the district is probably a non-negotiable for you. However, in terms of the purpose of assessing students in PA, using "best practices" in assessment suggests that determining where a student is and making appropriate instructional adjustments should be the priorities. Clearly, it is beneficial when the district requirements correlate with what constitutes "best practices" for students.

Please go back and select another answer.

You chose C. Glad to see you have such a good sense of humor—essential in the teaching profession. Keep smiling as you go back and select another answer.

Activities

One of These Sounds Is Not Like the Other

SKILL:
Listening (prerequisite for PA acquisition)

NUMBER OF STUDENTS:
Whole class, direct instruction

MATERIALS:
Whistle; two pencils

DIRECTIONS:

1. Make a series of three sounds that are all alike. Example: Clap three times; tap a pencil three times; blow a whistle three times. After each series of three, ask the children if the three sounds were alike.

2. Tell the children you are going to make three sounds again, but this time one of them will be different. They will have to figure out which one is different.

3. Blow the whistle once and tap two pencils together twice. Ask the children to identify the different sound.

4. Clap twice and pretend-sneeze once. Ask the children to identify the different sound.

5. Stomp your feet once, clap once, and stomp your feet once again. Ask the children to identify the different sound.

6. Say "s-s-s-s, moo, s-s-s-s." Ask the children to identify the different sound.

VARIATION:

Add some challenge by using the same sound all three times, but vary the number of times you make the sound. Example: Clap once; clap once; clap twice. Ask the children to identify which sound was different. Another example might be to toot the whistle twice in a row, then once, then once again. Ask the children to identify which sound was different.

Listen Up

SKILL:
Listening (prerequisite for PA acquisition)

NUMBER OF STUDENTS:
Small group (4–6 students)

MATERIALS:
Students' choice

DIRECTIONS:

1. Ask the group to close their eyes. Snap your fingers three times. Ask the group to open their eyes and tell you what they heard.

2. Tell the students you are going to play a listening game. Divide the group into two teams.

3. Tell each team to come up with a sound they can all make together. Remind them of the example you used—snapping your fingers. They may make any sound they want, and they may use items located around the room to help make the sound.

4. When you call on a team, they make the sound while members of the second team close their eyes. After the first team finishes making the sound, the second team tries to guess what the sound was.

VARIATIONS:

1. Ask the team that had their eyes closed to try to re-create the sound they heard.

2. As a "wave of sound" energizer, ask each team to stand, make their sound, and sit back down.

Guess the Bigger Word

SKILL:
Concept of spoken word
(distinguishing word lengths)

NUMBER OF STUDENTS:
Small group (4–6 students)

MATERIALS:
Construction paper or cardstock rectangles of two different sizes—2" × 3" and 2" × 6"
(Each child needs one of each size.)

DIRECTIONS:

1. Tell the children that they are going to play a listening game. They will listen to two words and then decide which one is longer.

2. Say the words *bed* and *caterpillar*. Ask them to tell you which word they think is longer.

3. When they agree that *caterpillar* is the longer word, show them two paper or cardstock rectangles—one longer than the other. Ask which shape they think would be *bed* and which shape would be *caterpillar*. Reinforce the idea that the shorter one would be *bed* because *bed* is the shorter word.

4. Ask one child to say "bed" and another to say "caterpillar." Tell them to both say their word at the same time after you say "go." Ask the rest of the group to listen to see which child finishes his/her word last. That person finishes last because he/she has a longer word to say.

5. Give each child one long and one short rectangle shape. Say the word *bed*. Ask the group to hold up the shape they think would be *bed*. Ask them to hold up the shape they think would be *caterpillar*. Each time, ask them why they made the decision to hold up that particular shape.

6. Possible word pairs to use:
    ant – blackboard
    happy – a
    decide – the
    fat – gigantic
    ridiculous – kind
    dinosaur – dog

Push-a-Word

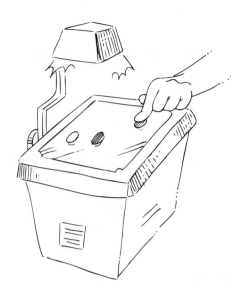

SKILL:
Concept of spoken word (sentence segmentation)

NUMBER OF STUDENTS:
Whole class, direct instruction

MATERIALS:
Five manipulatives, such as colored chips,
Unifix cubes, or counters

DIRECTIONS:

1. Tell the students you are going to show them how to make a sentence using counters on the overhead projector.

2. Start out with a short sentence, such as "I like cake."

3. Say the sentence again, and this time push up a counter as you say each word. Leave about two inches between each counter.

4. Point to the last counter and call on a student to tell you which word that counter represents. Point to the first counter and ask a student to tell you which word that counter represents. Point to the middle counter and ask a student to tell you which word that counter represents.

5. Use the same procedure using longer sentences with one-syllable words.

6. If the children are having success with this activity, add sentences with two-syllable words, such as "Today is Tuesday." Build up to sentences with three-syllable words.

VARIATIONS:

1. Have the children clap the words for each sentence.

2. Call four students up to the front of the room and have them stand shoulder to shoulder. Assign them each a different word in a sentence, such as "Nick has brown eyes." Say the sentence slowly and have each student take a step forward when his/her word is called.

Rhyme-a-Word

SKILL:
Rhyme recognition

NUMBER OF STUDENTS:
Whole class, direct instruction

MATERIALS:
List of rhyming words below

"boy" - "toy"   "hit" - "sack"

DIRECTIONS:

1. Tell the students to stand up.

2. Inform them that they are going to play a rhyming game. They have to listen for words that sound alike at the end. Tell them you are going to say two words, and they are to decide if they rhyme or not. If they rhyme, then they are to bow. If they do not rhyme, they are to raise their arms over their head.

3. Give some examples first. Try boy – toy. They rhyme, so the children should all bow. Try hit – sack. They do not rhyme, so the children should raise their arms.

4. Suggested word sets to use:
   go – toe
   bat – cat
   run – tan
   itch –pitch
   house – mouse
   big – bag
   star – car

5. Honor those students who need some extra processing time by saying the two words while holding out your arm with palm down and then telling the children they are not to do anything until you drop your arm.

VARIATIONS:

1. Students clap once if the words rhyme, and they remain silent if they do not rhyme.

2. Students say "salami, pastrami" if they rhyme and say "no way" if they do not rhyme.

Smiley Wiley and Sad Sarah

SKILL:
Rhyme recognition

NUMBER OF STUDENTS:
Whole class, direct instruction

MATERIALS:
Tongue depressors or craft sticks

DIRECTIONS:

1. Distribute the sticks and have the children draw a happy face on the top part of one side and a sad face on the top of the back side. (Children can put stickers on instead if they wish.) Name the happy face "Smiley Wiley" and the sad face "Sad Sarah."

2. Tell the children you are going to say two words at a time. They have to decide whether they rhyme or not. If they rhyme, they hold up "Smiley Wiley." If they do not rhyme, they hold up "Sad Sarah."

3. Possible word sets to use:
    bet – get
    go – me
    fan – pan
    gold – back
    cake – take
    big – dig
    cash – cup
    dust – must

VARIATION:

Say a word and have students guess a pseudoword, or nonsense word, that rhymes with your word. Examples: rake – dake, pig – kig.

Complete a Rhyme for Forgetful Freddy

SKILL:
Rhyme completion

NUMBER OF STUDENTS:
Whole class, direct instruction, or with partners

MATERIALS:
Rhyming couplets (below)

DIRECTIONS:

1. Tell the students that Forgetful Freddy can't remember the ending to these sentences. Ask the students if they can help Freddy by completing each sentence with a rhyming word.

2. Say each couplet, leaving out the last word and letting the children complete it.

> The airplane can fly
> high in the _____. (sky)

> I saw a mouse
> run in the _____. (house)

> Mother will bake
> a big birthday _____. (cake)

> I had a good dream.
> I ate some ice _____. (cream)

> I was fast on my feet
> as I ran down the _____. (street)

> Look at the bear
> with the brown, furry _____. (hair)

VARIATIONS:

1. Have the girls answer the first one, the boys answer the second one, and so on.

2. Have the children get with a partner and agree on the answers. Then call on a pair to answer each one.

Draw a Rhyme a Line at a Time

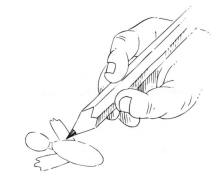

SKILL:
Rhyme completion

NUMBER OF STUDENTS:
Whole class, direct instruction

MATERIALS:
Rhyming couplets (below)

DIRECTIONS:

1. Tell the children that they are going to hear a funny story about a friendly creature named Ed. They are going to draw Ed a little at a time as you read the rhyming story below. Read two lines of the rhyming story at a time and leave out the underlined rhyming word each time.

2. Tell the children that they have to figure out the word, say the word out loud, and then draw it.

> Once there was a creature named Ed.
> He started out with a great big <u>head</u>.
>
> He won't be a nervous wreck
> if you give this creature a <u>neck</u>.
>
> Because he likes to do karate,
> let us give him a nice big <u>body</u>.
>
> Even though he'll do no harm,
> on each side he needs an <u>arm</u>.
>
> Since it's hard to walk on wooden pegs,
> Let's give our creature two long <u>legs</u>.
>
> Now our Ed is finally done.
> Wasn't that a lot of <u>fun</u>?

VARIATION:

Read the story and have one child at a time come up to the board and draw the item that depicts the missing word.

What's in the Bag?

SKILL:
Rhyme production

NUMBER OF STUDENTS:
Whole class, direct instruction

MATERIALS:
Bag filled with 10 recognizable items, such as dice, ball, pencil, ribbon, book, plastic or real apple, paper clip, safety pin, ruler, shoe

DIRECTIONS:

1. Tell the children that you have a bag filled with items they have seen before. One child at a time gets to pick an object out of the bag and say what it is. Then he/she has to say a word that rhymes with that object. It is OK to say a nonsense word if it rhymes. Example: If the ball is picked, an appropriate rhyming word would be *wall*. An appropriate nonsense word would be *vall*.

2. Add an optional element of fun by deciding who picks by using one or more of these qualifiers:

    The person who can say a word that rhymes with his/her name
    The person whose birthday is closest to today
    The person whose last name begins with the sound /b/
    The person who knows the name of our vice president
    The person who can tell the class what a syllable is
    The person who can think of a long word

Make up as many as you want.

Note:

For objects that have two-word names, such as *safety pin*, the child should come up with a rhyming word for just the second word—in this case, *pin*.

Rhyme-a-Card

SKILL:
Rhyme production

NUMBER OF STUDENTS:
Small group (4–6 students)

MATERIALS:
Deck of playing cards (Take out half the deck, leaving two of everything instead of four of everything.)

"Jack" = "back"

DIRECTIONS:

1. Tell the children they are going to play a rhyming game.

2. Call on a student volunteer who wants to play first. Fan out the cards face-down on a table in front of the student.

3. Ask the student to pick a card. Once he/she has picked one, tell him/her to think of a word that rhymes with the number or picture on the card. If the child picks a 2–10, he/she thinks of a word that rhymes with the number picked. If the child picks an ace or picture card, he/she thinks of a word that rhymes with the word *jack, queen, king,* or *ace.*

4. Once the student says a rhyming word, he/she puts the card in the center of the table.

5. If the student cannot think of a real word that rhymes, he/she may say a pseudoword, or nonsense word.

VARIATIONS:

1. A student chooses a card, holds it up, and calls on someone to think of a word that rhymes with the number or picture on the card.

2. Put the cards face-down on the table. The first student picks a card and holds it up. He/she thinks of a word that rhymes with the number or picture on the card and passes the card to the right. The next student has to think of another rhyming word. Each time a student says a rhyming word, the other students have to indicate agreement or disagreement by a thumbs up or a thumbs down.

Silly Attendance

SKILL:
Syllable blending

NUMBER OF STUDENTS:
Whole class, direct instruction

MATERIALS:
None

DIRECTIONS:

1. Tell the students you are going to take attendance in a silly way. Call out the students' names by segmenting the syllables in their names. Example: Su-san, Sa-man-tha, Fred-dy. For one-syllable names, just say the name; for example, Todd.

2. Tell the students that when they hear their name called, they stand up and say their name normally. Example: Su-san would be Susan, Sa-man-tha would be Samantha, and so on. A student with a one-syllable name would just stand up and say his/her name.

VARIATION:

A more challenging version might involve your saying a student's name and the student's saying his/her name and the number of syllables in it. Example: You say "Sa-man-tha." Samantha stands up and says "Samantha—three."

In the phonological awareness literature, *blending* is sometimes referred to as *synthesis*.

Get Your Blenders Out

SKILL:
Syllable blending

NUMBER OF STUDENTS:
Whole class, direct instruction

MATERIALS:
List of words below

DIRECTIONS:

1. Tell the students you are going to say some words in a very strange way. Ask them to figure out what word you are trying to say. Start by segmenting compound words. Pause for about a second between syllables. Below are some examples.

    sun – shine
    book – case
    shoe –box
    air – plane
    birth – day
    foot – ball

2. Tell the students you are going to say some harder words now. Use words that are not compound words. Remind the children they have to be good detectives and good listeners to figure out these words. Some examples include:

    hap – py
    win – dow
    lit – tle
    scis – sors
    sur – prise
    tel – e – phone
    di – no – saur

VARIATION:

Inform the students that they are going to pretend their arms are blenders. Each arm will stand for one syllable of a word. For the word *popcorn*, put one arm out to the side with a fist at the end and say "pop." Leaving the first arm up, put the second one out to the side with a fist at the end and say "corn." Then put both arms together and blend the word, saying "popcorn."

"pop"   "corn"   "popcorn"

 Activities

Paper-Plate Syllables

SKILL:
Syllable segmentation

NUMBER OF STUDENTS:
Small group (4–6 students)

MATERIALS:
Pictures of objects depicting two-, three-, and four-syllable words; four paper plates

DIRECTIONS:

1. Have the children sit in a circle on the floor. Put four paper plates in a horizontal row on the floor in the middle of the circle.

2. Show the children a picture of an object depicting a two-, three-, or four-syllable word.

3. Ask a volunteer to come into the middle of the circle and push up (i.e., slide on the floor), one at a time, the number of paper plates matching the number of syllables in the word. The student should say each syllable while pushing each plate up. Example: For the word *alligator*, the student would push up all four plates, saying one of the syllables for each plate (al–li–ga–tor).

4. Wait until the student is finished and then have the rest of the children clap the syllables in the word to see if the answer is correct.

VARIATION:

Put two paper plates in the middle of the circle and ask the students to think of words with two syllables. For a real challenge, put three paper plates in the middle of the circle and ask the students to think of three-syllable words. Give clues if necessary. Example: "I'm thinking of a three-syllable word. It's a large animal, and it has a trunk." (Answer: elephant.)

The Syllable Game

SKILL:
Syllable segmentation

NUMBER OF STUDENTS:
Whole class, direct instruction

MATERIALS:
None

DIRECTIONS:

1. Have students choose partners.

2. Ask each pair to say their names to each other and decide how many syllables there are in each of their names.

3. Tell each pair to decide who will be number 1 and who will be number 2.

4. Teach the class this cheer:

> Let's all play the syllable game.
> How many parts in your friend's name?
> Clap all the parts that you can hear.
> If you're right, you'll get a cheer.

5. Choose one pair to come up to the front of the room. Have person 1 say the following:
   This is my friend.
   His/her name is _____.

6. Have the rest of the class say the cheer in step 4.

7. Ask person 1 to clap the syllables in his/her friend's name and to tell the class the number of syllables clapped.

8. If the answer is correct, everybody cheers. If the answer is incorrect, the teacher and the class encourage correction by clapping the name together.

9. Then person 2 says:
   This is my friend.
   His/her name is _____.

10. Repeat steps 6–8.

Where Has My Little Part Gone?

SKILL:
Syllable deletion with compound words

NUMBER OF STUDENTS:
Whole class, direct instruction

MATERIALS:
None

DIRECTIONS:

1. Tell the children you will be singing a song about word parts that are missing. You will be singing to the tune of "Where, Oh, Where Has My Little Dog Gone?" The children will have to figure out what word parts are left. The first word is *cowboy*.

> Where, oh, where has my little part gone?
> Oh, where, oh, where can it be?
> I lost the *cow*, and I have one part left,
> And now I'm alone known as _____. (boy)

2. The next word is *playground*.

> Where, oh, where has my little part gone?
> Oh, where, oh, where can it be?
> I lost the *ground*, and I have one part left,
> And alone I'm known as _____. (play)

3. Additional compound words to use: inside, outside, snowman, airplane, flashlight, doorbell, bedroom, haircut, cookbook.

VARIATION:

Have two children come up to the front of the room.
Have two chairs up in front, one for each child.
Tell each child one part of a compound word.
Example: One child is *foot*, and the other child is *ball*.
Then you say, "Say *football* without *ball*." The child with *foot* should stand up and say "foot."

The Syllable Thief

SKILL:
Syllable deletion

NUMBER OF STUDENTS:
Whole class, direct instruction

MATERIALS:
Puppet to play the Syllable Thief

DIRECTIONS:

1. Tell the children that a thief has been stealing parts of words. Use a puppet that you already have and put a sign around it that says "Syllable Thief."

2. Tell the children that you have made friends with the Syllable Thief, and he tells you secrets. The secrets are the parts of the words he steals. The children have to act as word detectives and figure out what parts are left.

3. Have the puppet whisper in your ear. Tell the students that the Syllable Thief told you he came across the word *pencil* and stole *pen*. Ask the "detectives" to figure out what part of the word is left (*cil*).

4. Have the Syllable Thief whisper in your ear again. Tell the students that the Syllable Thief told you he came across the word *hammer* and stole *mer*. Ask them to figure out what part of the word is left (*ham*).

5. Other two-syllable words you could use include *balloon, water, dinner, insect, exclaim, surprise, pumpkin,* and *flavor*. Alternate between the Syllable Thief's stealing the first part of a word and the second part.

6. Make a pretend jail and choose a "Sheriff" to put the Syllable Thief in jail for whatever period of time he/she thinks is appropriate. Ask the children to brainstorm ways in which the Syllable Thief can act legally, such as by borrowing parts of words or asking first before taking them.

VARIATION:

Make the game challenging by adding some three-syllable words, such as *kangaroo, bicycle, forever,* and *vacation*. Have the Syllable Thief take off the first or last syllable, and let the children guess what is left.

Jack-in-the-Box

SKILL:
Phoneme isolation of initial sound

NUMBER OF STUDENTS:
Whole class, direct instruction

MATERIALS:
None

DIRECTIONS:

Tell the students that they are going to be
like a jack-in-the-box. Say a word, and the students
jump up if their name begins with the first sound of
the word you said. Example: Say the word
toy. Terri, Tameika, and Thomas jump up.

Note:

You may have to help those children whose names
begin with a consonant cluster, such as Stan.
He stands up when he hears /s/. Students whose
names begin with a digraph, such as Sharon
and Chad, should stand when they hear /sh/ and /ch/, respectively.
Make sure you use words that allow all the children to have a turn.

VARIATION:

To the tune of "If You're Happy and You Know It," have the students respond accordingly:

If your name begins with /t/, stand up.
If your name begins with /t/, stand up.
If your name begins with /t/, stand up and wave your hands.
If your name begins with /t/, stand up.

Name the First Sound That You Hear

SKILL:
Phoneme isolation of initial sound

NUMBER OF STUDENTS:
Whole group, direct instruction

MATERIALS:
None

DIRECTIONS:

1. Sing this song to the tune of "Clementine." Have the children call out the first sound of the word according to the song's instructions.

> Listen, children, listen, children,
> As I say a word out loud.
> Guess the first sound that it starts with,
> And you'll all feel very proud.
>
> The word is *boat*. [Say this line. Do not sing it.]
>
> What's the sound that you all hear
> At the start of the word *boat*?
> Listen, children, name the first sound
> That you hear in the word *boat*.

2. The children call out "/b/."

3. Other words to use in the song: dog, car, mouse, voice, town, peach, not.

VARIATIONS:

1. Ask the children to give you new words to put in the song.

2. Ask those children whose names begin with the first sound of the target word to stand at the end of the song.

Eddie Ending

SKILL:
Phoneme isolation of final sound

NUMBER OF STUDENTS:
Whole class, direct instruction

MATERIALS:
Finger puppet you have named Eddie Ending

DIRECTIONS:

1. Decide which final sounds to concentrate on for this activity. Find pictures of items that end with those sounds.

2. Hold up two pictures—one of an item ending with the first targeted sound, and the other of an item ending with a sound not targeted. For example, if the targeted sound is /k/, you might hold up a picture of a duck. The other picture might be of a bat.

3. Call on a child to put Eddie Ending on his/her finger and then have Eddie point to the picture of the item that has the targeted sound.

4. Ask the students to tell you why Eddie did not point to the other picture.

5. Repeat steps 2–4 for the other targeted sounds.

VARIATION:

Give small groups of four children approximately 12 pictures. Have them sort the pictures by ending sound into columns. For example, you can have some pictures of items that end with /k/ and some of items that end with /l/. You can have a third column for "other," which would include any pictures of items that end with neither /k/ nor /l/.

Final-Sound Picture Sort

SKILL:
Phoneme isolation of final sound

NUMBER OF STUDENTS:
Small group (2–4 students)

MATERIALS:
Pictures of objects depicting words
to sort for final sounds

DIRECTIONS:

1. Tell the students to sort the pictures into two rows going side-ways or two columns going up and down. One row or column should have all the pictures of objects depicting words that end with the sound /t/. The other should have all the pictures of objects depicting words that end with the sound /k/.

2. Find pictures of objects depicting the following suggested words: back, bat, fork, mat, clock, belt, meat, pink, plant, vest, snake, wallet, duck, skirt, skunk, coat, chalk.

VARIATION:

Use this variation with the whole class. Choose two children to come up to the front of the room. Give one child a picture of an object depicting a word that ends with the sound /k/ and the other child a picture of an object depicting a word that ends with the sound /t/. Pass out the rest of the pictures—one per child. Have one child at a time come up and say the last sound of the object in the picture he/she is holding. Then that child stands in front of the person who is holding a picture of an object that ends with the same sound. The rest of the children indicate agreement or disagreement with that child's choice by a thumbs up or a thumbs down. Continue until all the children are standing in front of the right person.

Think Sounds

SKILL:
Isolation of initial and final sounds

NUMBER OF STUDENTS:
Small group (4–6 students)

MATERIALS:
None

DIRECTIONS:

1. Sit in a circle. Start by saying a word, such as *goat*, to the children. Tell them that the child sitting next to you has to think of a word that starts with the last sound of the word you just said. Since the last sound of *goat* is /t/, that child must think of a word that starts with /t/.

2. Let's say the child says "tooth." The next child has to come up with a word that starts with /th/. An example might be *thank*.

3. The important thing to remember is to think sounds, not letters. Here is a sample round: goat, teeth, thank, kitten, nice, sat, took, kangaroo, ooze, zebra, about, tap, pan, neck, catch, cheat, time, money, enough. Remember that sometimes the letter that ends a word is not the last sound of that word.

Think sounds, not letters.

Push It Up

SKILL:
Isolation of initial, medial, and final sounds

NUMBER OF STUDENTS:
Small group (4–6 students)

MATERIALS:
Three connected boxes for each child (see reproducible on next page); three manipulatives or counters for each child

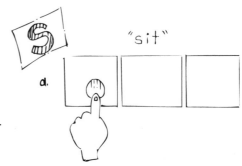

"sit"

d.

DIRECTIONS:

1. Give each child a picture of three connected boxes* and three counters.

2. Tell the children that they are going to play a game with their counters. Have them put one counter under each box.

3. Decide on a targeted sound; for example, /s/.

4. Tell the children that some words begin with the /s/ sound, some have the /s/ sound in the middle, and some end with the /s/ sound.

"hissing"

b.

5. Tell them that you will say a word. If the word begins with the /s/ sound, they are to push the counter up into the first box. If the word ends with the /s/ sound, they are to push the counter up into the last box. If the word has the /s/ sound in the middle, they are to push the counter up into the middle box.

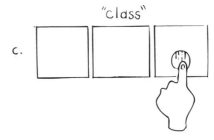

"class"

c.

6. Possible words to include for the /s/ sound are *sit, class, hissing, this, passing,* and *sand.*

VARIATION:

Have three children stand in front of the room. Have one child represent the initial sound, one child the medial sound, and one child the final sound. Decide on the targeted sound. Let's say you choose /d/. If you say "do," the child representing the initial sound should take one step forward. The rest of the class can indicate agreement or disagreement with a thumbs up or a thumbs down. If the class agrees, the child steps back in line, and you give another word. The child representing the place in the word where the sound is heard steps forward, and so forth.

*These boxes are called Elkonin boxes in honor of D.B. Elkonin, the Russian psychologist who developed them.

68

Sing a Rhyme with Onset and Rime

SKILL:
Phoneme blending of onset and rime
(Note: *Onset* is the first consonant or
consonant blend in a word; *rime*, which is spelled
the old English way, without the *h* and with
an *i* instead of a *y*, is the first vowel of a word plus
all the letters that follow it. The concept of onset and rime
is the same as that of word families, or phonograms.)

NUMBER OF STUDENTS:
Whole class, direct instruction

MATERIALS:
None

DIRECTIONS:

1. Tell the children they will be playing a game in which they put sounds together to make a word. They will try to figure out each word to the tune of "If You're Happy and You Know It," as in the example below.

> If you're happy and you know it, say my name: /c/ /ake/.
> If you're happy and you know it, say my name: /c/ /ake/.
> If you're happy and you know it, then your face will surely show it.
> If you're happy and you know it, say my name.
> (Children in unison say "cake.")

2. Other words to use: /b/ /oy/, /h/ /at/, /sh/ /op/, /ch/ /in/, /b/ /ack/, /s/ /it/.

VARIATIONS:

1. You may want to call this variation "Speedo." Say an onset/rime, such as /l/ /ock/, and have the children say "lock." Then do another one, such as /g/ /old/, and have the children say "gold." Keep saying an onset/rime and have the children say the whole word. Start to speed up and continue to get faster and faster.

2. Play a guessing game with the children. Say, "I'm thinking of a word. It starts with /b/. It ends with /at/. Can you guess the word?" Sample onsets and rimes to use: /t/ /ack/, /c/ /ash/, /t/ /an/, /p/ /each/, /m/ /eat/, /pl/ /ay/.

Tap to the Rhythm

SKILL:
Phoneme blending of onset and rime

NUMBER OF STUDENTS:
Whole class, direct instruction

MATERIALS:
Two sticks or pencils per child

DIRECTIONS:

1. Give two sticks or pencils to each child.

2. Tell the children they are to tap their sticks or pencils on their desks once when they say the beginning part of a word and once when they say the ending part of a word. For example, for /b/ /ack/, the children would tap once while saying /b/ and tap once again while saying /ack/.

3. Next, tell the children to tap their pencils together and say the whole word *back*. The three taps should be without pauses in between. It sounds like "tap, tap, tap" while they say "/b/, /ack/, back."

4. Words to use: /ack/ family—back, tack, rack, sack, knack, Jack; /ed/ family—bed, fed, led, Ned, red, Ted. Use onsets and rimes that are in the students' present literature or poetry.

VARIATION:

Start by saying words that are in the same word family (i.e., they have the same rime). As the children get good at the rhythm, make it more challenging by giving words from different word families or adding words that begin with a consonant cluster.

Read My Mind

SKILL:
Phoneme blending of onset and rime

NUMBER OF STUDENTS:
Whole class, direct instruction

MATERIALS:
None

DIRECTIONS:

1. Say the following verse in a chant or rhythm. If you want, clap your hands or snap your fingers while you are saying it.

> I'm thinking of a word.
> It ends with /ack/.
> It starts with /b/.
> The word is _____. (back)

2. Continue the same rhythm, using new onsets and rimes. Have the children say the last word of the verse.

3. Other onsets and rimes to use:
   at – /s/ – sat
   ake – /c/ – cake
   en – /t/ – ten
   ide – /r/ – ride
   in – /p/ – pin
   ot – /d/ – dot

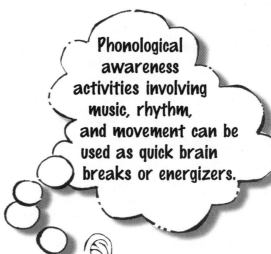

Phonological awareness activities involving music, rhythm, and movement can be used as quick brain breaks or energizers.

Guess the Word

SKILL:
Phoneme blending

NUMBER OF STUDENTS:
Whole class, direct instruction

MATERIALS:
None

DIRECTIONS:

1. Ask three children to come up to the front of the room. They all sit down facing the rest of the class.

2. Using a three-phoneme word, such as *mat*, give each child a sound from the word. Whisper "/m/" to the first child, "/a/" to the second child, and "/t/" to the third child.

3. The first child stands up and says "/m/" and sits back down. The second child stands and says "/a/" and sits back down. The third child stands and says "/t/" and sits back down.

4. The rest of the class then says the entire word together: "mat."

5. Other words to use: /c/ /o/ /t/, /r/ /u/ /g/, /sh/ /i/ /p/, /ch/ /i/ /n/, /f/ /a/ /n/.

VARIATION:

Put some pictures in a bag. Have one child at a time pull one picture out of the bag and show it to you. If a child shows you a picture of a pig, for instance, you say to the rest of the children, "I see a /p/ /i/ /g/." The children have to guess what's in the picture.

I'm Thinking of a Word

SKILL:
Phoneme blending

NUMBER OF STUDENTS:
Whole class, direct instruction

MATERIALS:
None

DIRECTIONS:

1. Sing this song to the tune of "The Wheels on the Bus."

The teacher sings,

"I'm thinking of a word named /m/ /a/ /n/, /m/ /a/ /n/, /m/ /a/ /n/.
I'm thinking of a word named /m/ /a/ /n/.
What is my word?"

The students sing back,

"Are you thinking of the word called man, man, man,
Man, man, man, man, man, man?
Are you thinking of the word called man, man, man?"

The teacher sings,

"Yes, *man* is my word."

2. Other suggested words to use in the song: cap, bus, tin, rock, set.

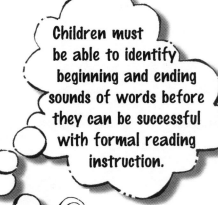

Children must be able to identify beginning and ending sounds of words before they can be successful with formal reading instruction.

Hippity Hop

SKILL:
Phoneme segmentation

NUMBER OF STUDENTS:
Small group (4–6 students)

MATERIALS:
Four connected boxes per child
(see reproducible on next page)
for the variation of this activity

DIRECTIONS:

1. Tell the students they get to hop like frogs while doing this activity.

2. Orally, give each student a word. One at a time, each child says his/her word and hops as many times as there are sounds in the word. Example: For the word *bed*, the child hops three times. With every hop, the student says the sound of each phoneme.

3. Sample words to use: cup, bite, pass, ship, blue, nest, give.

VARIATION:

Give each child four connected boxes and four counters. Say a word, and the students push up a counter for each sound they hear in the word. Share answers.

Tap-a-Sound

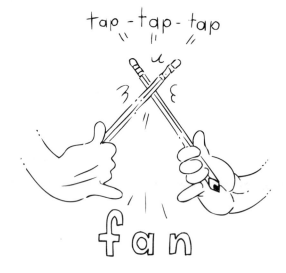

SKILL:
Phoneme segmentation

NUMBER OF STUDENTS:
Small group (6 students)

MATERIALS:
One pencil for each child

DIRECTIONS:

1. Have students choose partners.

2. Tell the students you are going to play a sound-counting game. You will say a word, and each pair will tap their pencils together as many times as there are sounds in the word. For example, *fan* would have three taps.

3. After the children have tapped each word, ask one pair of students to demonstrate, and the other pairs indicate agreement or disagreement with a thumbs up or a thumbs down.

4. Possible words to use: it, hat, bake, ship, pen, fan, key, bag, rain, club.

VARIATION:

Give each student two paper plates. Tell the students to brush their plates together for each sound they hear in the word you say.

Twinkle, Twinkle, Little Word

SKILL:
Phoneme deletion of initial sound

NUMBER OF STUDENTS:
Whole class, direct instruction

MATERIALS:
None

DIRECTIONS:

1. Tell the children you are going to teach them a song that will help them discover new words that are inside bigger words.

2. Sing this song to the tune of "Twinkle, Twinkle, Little Star." Let them fill in the last word of each verse.

Twinkle, twinkle, little word,
What's the new word to be heard?
If I take off the first sound,
What new word will now be found?
Take the /p/ right off of *pout*.
Now the new word sounds like _____. (out)

Twinkle, twinkle, little word,
What's the new word to be heard?
If I take off the first sound,
What new word will now be found?
Take the /c/ right off of *cold*.
Now the new word sounds like _____. (old)

3. After a few verses using new words, invite the children to sing along. Other possible words to use: bus, meat, sled, hand, fit, win, ball, farm, boat.

VARIATION:

Vary the calling out of the new word by calling on just the girls, then just the boys, or calling on a student sitting on one side of the room, then one sitting on the other side.

Name That Word

SKILL:
Phoneme deletion of initial sound

NUMBER OF STUDENTS:
Whole class, direct instruction

MATERIALS:
None

DIRECTIONS:

1. Choose two volunteers to come up to the front of the room.

2. Divide the word *give* into onset and rime (i.e., word family). Whisper "/g/" to the first child and "/iv/" to the second child.

3. The volunteer who has /g/ steps forward and says "/g/" and then steps back. The second volunteer steps forward, says "/iv/," and stays there.

4. After the second child says "/iv/," ask the rest of the class to name the nonsense word that is left after you take off the /g/. Create some excitement by shouting, "Name that word!"

5. Choose two new volunteers to come up to the front of the room and repeat the process. Other suggested words to use: house, barn, bell, tap, did, horse, good, must, sing, jump.

VARIATION:

Make it more challenging by using words that begin with a consonant blend or digraph, such as *spill, stop, blue, frog, clap, stick, chip, shop,* and *thick*. Remember, the consonant blend is the onset, and the rime is the first vowel and all the letters that follow; for instance, /sp/ /ill/ and /th/ /ick/.

Mr. Smart's Smart Idea

SKILL:
Phoneme deletion of final sound

NUMBER OF STUDENTS:
Whole class, direct instruction

MATERIALS:
None

DIRECTIONS:

Tell the children the following story:

It was Monday evening, the night when all the words met and made up stories using themselves. Sometimes the stories were very funny, and Mr. Giggles rolled out of his chair, laughing. Sometimes the stories were very unhappy, and Mrs. Sad cried and cried.

Well, on this night Mr. Hot decided he was way too warm, and he wanted to cool off. He thought that if he took off his last sound, he'd feel cooler. But he didn't want to be the only one without his last sound. So he asked all his friends for help.

All the words liked Mr. Hot and were willing to do anything to help him. So they asked what he wanted them to do. He said, "I want to take off my last sound, and I would be so happy if the rest of you would take off your last sounds, too, so I won't be alone."

The words thought and thought about it. They weren't sure if it was a very good idea at all. But they really, really liked Mr. Hot and said they would try it for a while—all except Mr. Smart. He just didn't think it was a good idea. He thought there would be a problem, and he was right.

The problem was that they all became new words. For example, Ms. Mouse became Ms. Mou. Mr. Chin became Mr. Chi. Little Betty became Little Bet. Can you figure out what the other words became?

Mr. Stove without his /v/ became Mr. _____. (Sto)
Mrs. Block without her /k/ became Mrs. _____. (Blo)
Little Mop without her /p/ became Little _____. (Mo)
Mr. Pen without his /n/ became Mr. _____. (Pe)
Ms. Happy without her /e/ became Ms. _____. (Hap)
Little Liz without her /z/ became Little _____. (Li)
Her dog Spot without his /t/ became _____. (Spo)
Mrs. Bunny without her /e/ became Mrs. _____. (Bun)
Mr. Hot without his /t/ became Mr. _____. (Ho)

Well, needless to say, there was a lot of confusion. Once the words took off their final sounds, they didn't know who they were anymore. Ms. Hap didn't know she was supposed to be Ms. Happy, so she just stopped smiling. Mr. Sto didn't know he was supposed to be Mr. Stove, so he stopped cooking. Spo didn't know he was a dog and didn't know if he should bark or say "Moo."

They all went to Mr. Ho, who used to be Mr. Hot, and said, "Please, can we have our sounds back? We don't know what to do or who we really are without our final sounds. We want to help you, but we are all so confused. Please, Mr. Ho, let us have our sounds back."

Mr. Ho thought about it for a long time. He noticed that things just weren't the same anymore. Everyone was confused and not at all happy. Mr. Smart, who was a good problem-solver, had a great idea. He said, "Mr. Ho, why don't you put your final sound back on and take off your sweater instead?" Mr. Ho did just that and felt much cooler. He then told everyone else to put their final sounds back on. So,

Mr. Sto with his /v/ was now Mr. _____ (Stove), and he could cook.

Mrs. Blo with her /k/ was now Mrs. _____(Block), and she could build things.

Little Mo with her /p/ was now Little _____(Mop) and could clean things.

Mr. Pe with his /n/ was now Mr. _____(Pen) and could write things.

Ms. Hap with her /e/ was now Ms. _____(Happy), and she got her smile back.

Little Li with her /z/ was now Little _____(Liz), and her friends knew who she was.

Her dog Spo with his /t/ was now _____(Spot), and he could bury his bone.

Mrs. Bun with her /e/ was now Mrs. _____(Bunny), and she could run and hop.

Mr. Ho with his /t/ was now Mr. _____(Hot), and he felt really good because all his friends were happy again.

At their next meeting, the words gave Mr. Smart an award for his smart idea. Then they gave him a big cheer: "Hip, hip, hooray! Hip, hip, hooray! Hip, hip, _____ for Mr. Smart!" (Let the children shout the last *hooray*.)

Roll Away a Sound

SKILL:
Phoneme deletion of final sound

NUMBER OF STUDENTS:
Small group (6 students)

MATERIALS:
Ball

DIRECTIONS:

1. Have the students sit in a circle with you on the floor.

2. Tell the students they are going to play a game where they have to figure out the pretend or real word that is left after taking off the last sound of the word.

3. Roll the ball to the first student and say "bed." The student who receives the ball must say "be" (pronounced with a short *e*).

4. That student rolls the ball back to you, and you roll it to another student and say "rock." That student must say "ro" (pronounced with a short *o*).

5. That student rolls the ball back to you, and you continue the process until everyone has a turn. Each student continues to say the word you give without the final sound.

6. Possible words to use: can, top, fit, tack, nut, pass, take, feet.

VARIATION:

As you sit in a circle, say a word to the student sitting to your right. He/she says your word without the final sound. Then that same student says another word to the student to his/her right, and that student says that word without the final sound. Go all the way around the circle until everyone has had a turn.

Sound Away

SKILL:
Phoneme deletion of first sound in consonant blend

NUMBER OF STUDENTS:
Small group (4–6 students)

MATERIALS:
Copies of the reproducible pictures on the following pages; four counters per child

DIRECTIONS:

1. Give each student four counters and nine pictures with Elkonin boxes underneath (see reproducible pictures on pages 83–91).

2. Look at the picture of the tree. Have the students put one counter under each of the four boxes. Say the word *tree*. Tell the students to move their counters up, one at a time, for each sound they hear in the word *tree*. They should move up three counters (/t/ /r/ /e/).

3. Now tell them to remove the /t/ sound, so they should remove the first counter. Ask them what the new word or nonsense word is (*ree*).

4. Continue the process with the words for the other pictures: scale, truck, crowd, plug, clock, train, flag, globe.

VARIATION:

Make the nine pictures into transparencies to use on an overhead projector. Then you can do this activity with the whole class, using counters on the overhead. Call on different students to tell you the word or nonsense word that's left after you remove the first sound.

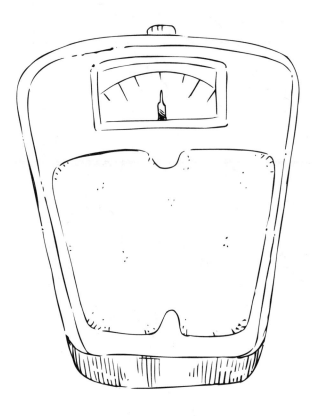

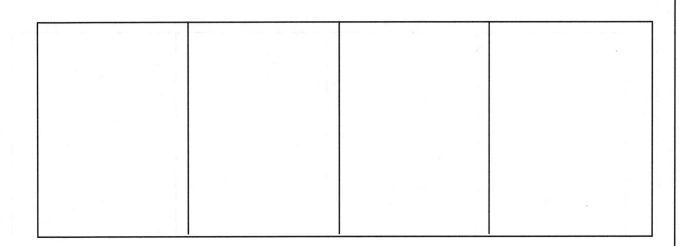

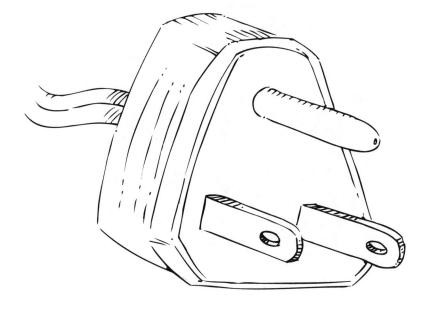

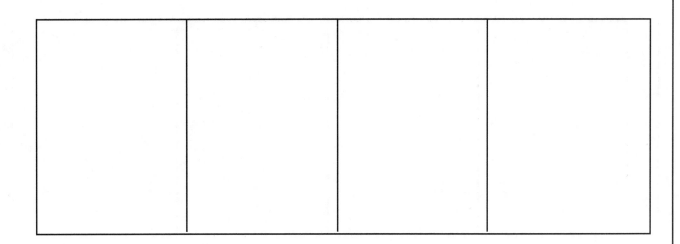

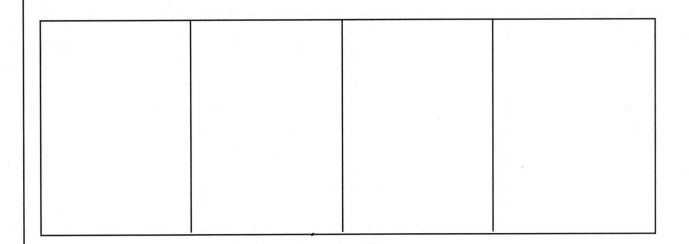

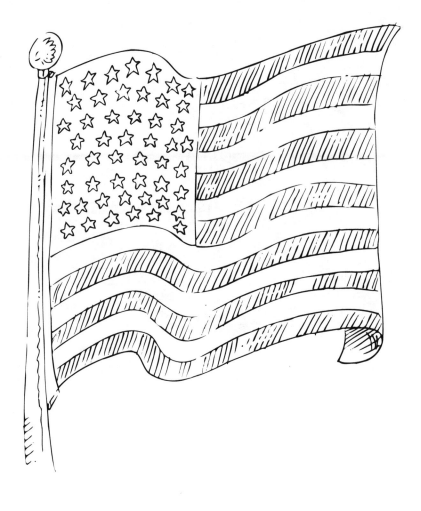

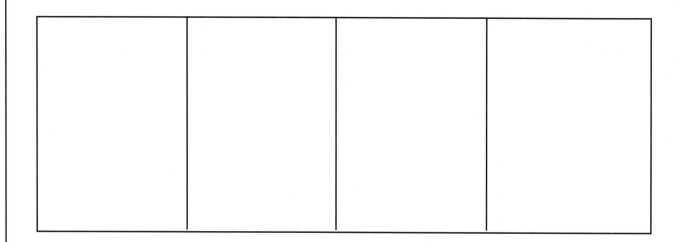

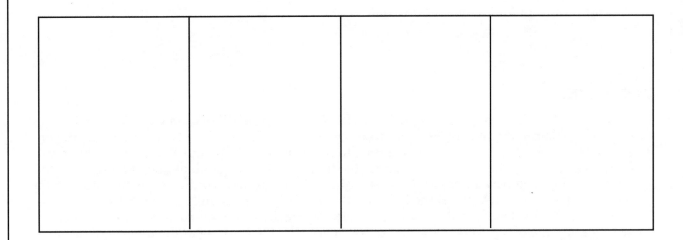

You're Out!

SKILL:
Phoneme deletion of first sound in consonant blend

NUMBER OF STUDENTS:
Whole class, direct instruction

MATERIALS:
None

DIRECTIONS:

1. Have the children stand up. Tell them you are going to say a word two times—once saying all the sounds in the word, and once taking off the first sound (example: *step, tep*). However, sometimes you will take off the first sound and say the rest of the word incorrectly.

2. Tell the students that if you say the word without the first sound correctly, they are to give the "safe" sign, as an umpire would do in a baseball game: start with arms crossed and pointed down, and then uncross them. When you say the word incorrectly, they are to give the "out" sign: hold one hand thumb-up, with arm bent at elbow; then lift arm and point upraised thumb over shoulder.

3. Sample words to use:

stop – top – safe	frog – fog – out
plane – lane – safe	tracks – racks – safe
glad – lad – safe	plum – lum – safe
clap – cap – out	blue – bue – out

VARIATION:

Make a baseball diamond on a magnetic board. Make two baseball players with little magnets on the back. (You can use the boy and girl from your school's Ellison die-cutting LetterMachine or trace any existing pattern.) Divide the class into two teams. "Throw" out a word and have the first student on the first team say it without the first sound. If the student does it correctly, his/her team's baseball player goes to first base. "Throw" out another word, and the first student on the second team says it without the first sound. If he/she is correct, his/her team's baseball player goes to first base. If a student says a word incorrectly, his/her team's player does not advance and the other team gets to try to say it correctly. Play as long as the interest holds up. (Make sure all the words you use start with a consonant blend.)

Cool Old MacDonald

SKILL:
Phoneme manipulation (addition of initial sound)

NUMBER OF STUDENTS:
Whole class, direct instruction

MATERIALS:
None

DIRECTIONS:

1. Teach the children this song to the tune of "Old MacDonald."

> Old MacDonald had a sound,
> And the sound was /at/.
> He put a /b/ in front of it,
> And now the word is _____. (bat)
> (Have the children say the word.)

> Old MacDonald had a sound,
> And the sound was /ed/.
> He put an /f/ in front of it,
> And now the word is _____. (fed)

> Old MacDonald had a sound,
> And the sound was /ock/.
> He put an /r/ in front of it,
> And now the word is _____. (rock)

2. Continue the song, making new words. Possible words to use:
   ame – /c/ – came
   ake – /t/ – take
   in – /p/ – pin
   et – /n/ – net
   ing – /k/ – king
   ad – /s/ – sad
   op – /ch/ – chop
   ip – /sh/ – ship
   end – /b/ – bend
   ish – /d/ – dish

Magic Words

SKILL:
Phoneme manipulation (addition of initial sound)

NUMBER OF STUDENTS:
Small group (4–6 students)

MATERIALS:
Magic wand

DIRECTIONS:

1. Tell the students they are going to do some magic tricks by making new words out of word endings.

2. The first word is *and*. Tell the students you are going to wave your magic wand to make *and* into a new word by adding the beginning sound /s/.

3. Say "/s/" while waving your magic wand in the air.

4. Ask the students the new word. (sand)

5. Give the wand to one of the students. Whisper a word ending, such as /eat/, and a word-beginning sound, such as /m/. Let the student be the "magician" by saying "/eat/" to the class and then waving the magic wand while saying "/m/." The other students guess the new word.

6. Other possible words for the "magicians" to use:

   at –/c/ – cat
   it – /l/ – lit
   ot – /d/ – dot
   ill – /f/ – fill
   eat – /m/ – meat
   arm – /f/ – farm
   ink – /s/ – sink
   out – /p/ – pout

Substitute, Bubstitute

SKILL:
Phoneme manipulation (substitution of initial sound)

NUMBER OF STUDENTS:
Whole class, direct instruction

MATERIALS:
None

"bead"

DIRECTIONS:

1. Sing the following songs on different days, with the children substituting a different beginning sound all the way through.

2. Sample songs to use:
Change "Head, shoulders, knees, and toes" to "Bead, boulders, bees, and bows." Do the motions with it.

Change "Zip-a-dee-doo-dah, zip-a-dee-ay" to "Lip-a-lee-loo-lah, lip-a-lee-lay."

Change "Fee-fi-fiddlio, fee-fi-fiddlio-o-o-o" to "Chee-chi-chiddlio, chee-chi-chiddlio-o-o-o."

3. You can use any song and simply substitute the beginning sounds with your own targeted sound for the day.

"boulders"

VARIATION:

Put each child's name on a slip of paper. Put all the papers in a container. Each day choose a child's name from the container. The first sound in that child's first name can be the sound for the day. During the day from time to time, sing a well-known song and substitute the beginning sounds of the words in the song with the beginning sound of that child's name.

"bees"

"boes"

Take Off and Put On

SKILL:
Phoneme manipulation (substitution of initial sound)

NUMBER OF STUDENTS:
Small group (4–6 students)

MATERIALS:
Pictures of objects depicting the words used in the activity
(If you are unable to find pictures of objects depicting the
words used, just say the words.)

DIRECTIONS:

1. Hold up a picture of a bug. Ask the children in the group to take
off the /b/ sound and add /t/. What is the new word? (tug)

2. Hold up a picture of a king. Take off the /k/ sound and add /r/.
What is the new word? (ring)

3. Continue with the following picture words and new sounds:

Picture Word	New Sound	New Word
ball	/f/	fall
wig	/p/	pig
mop	/t/	top
cup	/p/	pup
sack	/b/	back
sun	/r/	run
bee	/s/	see
leg	/b/	beg
pen	/t/	ten
sit	/l/	lit

VARIATION:

Give a picture to each of the students in the small group. The students take turns holding up
their pictures. For each picture's word, one student in the group substitutes a new initial sound
of his/her choice.

Silly Songs

SKILL:
Phoneme manipulation (substitution of initial sound)

NUMBER OF STUDENTS:
Whole class, direct instruction

MATERIALS:
Long pointer or fly swatter to be used as a "paddle"

DIRECTIONS:

1. Review the song "Row, Row, Row Your Boat."

2. Call a student to come up to the front of the class and give him/her the long pointer or fly swatter. The student will pretend to row a boat with this prop.

3. Have the class sing "Row, Row, Row Your Boat," but substitute the first sound in *row* and in *merrily* with the first sound of the student's name. For example, if his/her name is Sandy, the song would be sung like this:

   Sow, sow, sow your boat
   Gently down the stream.
   Serrily, serrily, serrily, serrily,
   Life is but a dream.

4. The other students can "row their boats" with their arms at their seats while singing the song.

> Fun phonological awareness activities promote Academic Learning Time (ALT), where children are actively engaged and meeting a 75% to 95% success rate.

Hi, Binda!

SKILL:
Phoneme manipulation
(substitution of initial sound)

NUMBER OF STUDENTS:
Whole class, direct instruction

MATERIALS:
None

DIRECTIONS:

1. Have the whole class stand in a big circle.

2. Tell the children they will be substituting the first sound in their names. Decide what sound you are going to substitute (example: /b/). Go around the circle as you follow the script below.

Teacher:	Boys and girls, this is Binda. (The name of the child next to you is Linda.)
Students:	Who?
Teacher:	Binda.
Students:	Oh, Binda. Hi, Binda.
Linda:	Boys and girls, this is Bevin. (The child's name is Kevin.)
Students:	Who?
Linda:	Bevin.
Students:	Oh, Bevin. Hi, Bevin.
Kevin:	(Continues the game.)

3. Go around the circle until everyone has a turn.

Note:

When substituting the /b/ sound, if a name begins with a digraph, such as Chuck, then the new name would be Buck. If a name begins with a consonant blend, such as Stan, then the new name would be Btan.

New Words in Color

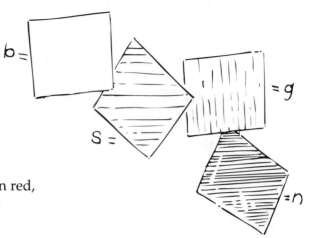

SKILL:
Phoneme manipulation
(substitution of final sound)

NUMBER OF STUDENTS:
Small group (4–6 students)

MATERIALS:
Construction paper squares (3" × 3") in red, blue, green, yellow, orange, and black

DIRECTIONS:

1. Give each student a different-colored square.

2. Tell the students that each color represents a different sound. They have to remember only their own sound.

red = /b/	yellow = /k/
blue = /t/	orange = /s/
green = /g/	black = /n/

3. Tell the students they are going to be replacing the last sound in the words you are going to call out. A new word will then be made for each word you call out.

4. Call out the word *bug* and then say "orange." The student with the orange card stands, holds up the orange card, which stands for /s/, and says, "*Bug* becomes *bus*."

5. Continue the activity, using the following suggested words and colors:

cap – blue – cat
kit – yellow – kick
cut – red – cub
hum – green – hug
pat – orange – pass
met – black – men
tug – red – tub
yes – blue – yet
duck – green – dug
bat – yellow – back
clap – orange – class
pet – black – pen

Clap if You Know

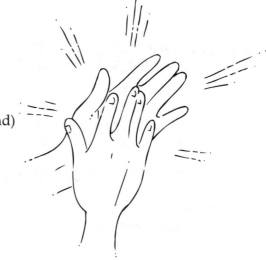

SKILL:
Phoneme manipulation (substitution of final sound)

NUMBER OF STUDENTS:
Small group (4–6 students)

MATERIALS:
None

DIRECTIONS:

1. Say a short word, such as *pan*. Then say "pad," substituting the final sound with /d/. The students have to figure out what sound you took off and what sound you added.

2. When a student thinks he/she knows the answer, he/she claps three times. Call on that student. If the answer is incorrect, another student may guess.

3. Tell the students that sometimes the new word will be a nonsense word.

4. So that everyone has an opportunity to think of the answer, allow some wait time after saying the two words. Tell the students they may not clap until after you clap once. Allow about five seconds to elapse before you clap.

Possible words and final-sound exchanges to use:

   pan – /d/ – pad
   club – /f/ – cluf
   mitt – /s/ – miss
   run – /g/ – rug
   hot – /p/ – hop
   men – /b/ – meb
   tape – /l/ – tale
   teen – /k/ – teek
   run – /j/ – ruj
   pin – /b/ – pib
   rake – /t/ – rate
   cat – /n/ – can

Phonological Awareness & Phonics Connection

Phonics & phonological awareness are inextricably woven together.

Phonics

Introducing the Alphabet

Recognizing the letters of the alphabet is an important prereading skill. Reciting the alphabet is usually much easier than actually naming the letters, which in turn is easier than knowing the letter sounds. Knowing the letter sounds is an essential skill for reading and spelling.

Introducing Consonants

On the subject of introducing new letters, researchers (Carnine, Silbert, and Kameenui, 1997) suggest several principles:

- Separate the introduction of letters that are visually confusing. For example, avoid introducing *b* and *d* or *p* and *q* together.

- Introduce only the most common sound for a new letter at first.

- Introduce more useful letters (such as *m* and *t*) before less useful ones (such as *x* and *q*).

- Possible introduction order of the alphabet: a, m, t, S/s, i, f, d, r, O/o, g, l, h, U/u, C/c, b, n, K/k, V/v, e, W/w, j, P/p, Y/y, T, L, M, F, D, I, N, A, R, H, G, B, X/x, q, Z/z, J, E, Q. Introduce identical uppercase and lowercase letters at the same time.

When preparing children for learning word blending, use words that begin with continuant sounds, such as /s/ and /f/, rather than words that begin with stop sounds, such as /t/ and /k/.

Systematic and Explicit Teaching of Phonics

Phonics instruction works best when it's built on a foundation of phonemic awareness and knowledge of how language works. It involves direct teaching of the most common sounds and their symbols, as well as instruction in blending the sounds together to pronounce words. Phonics lessons should include ample opportunities to practice the patterns being learned through the use of decodable text and engaging phonics games or activities. Involve students in word-building games regularly.

Sounding Out Words with Final Blending (Example: sat)

1. After writing *s* on the board, say the sound of the letter and then have the children say the sound with you.

2. Write *a* on the board, say the sound of the letter, and then have the children say the sound with you.

3. Blend the sounds while making a blending motion with your hand under the two letters and saying "sa."

4. Write *t* on the board, say the sound of the letter, and then have the children say the sound with you.

5. Blend the entire word, linking all the letter sounds together, while making a blending motion with your hand.

6. Have the children say the word and have a child use the word in a sentence.

Other Ways to Sound Out Words

- Successive blending: s, a, t
- Making the first sound and adding the rime (i.e., onset and rime): s, at, sat
- Backward chunking: at, s, sat
- Forward chunking: sa, t, sat

Lessons in Fabulous Phonics Format

1. Review the sound/letter correspondence previously taught. Introduce a short PA lesson with the phonics skill to be taught now.

   a. Review the previous phonics lesson.

   b. Introduce the digraph /sh/ by using a puppet named Shelly that has a mouth that opens and closes. Tell the students Shelly likes only those foods that have the /sh/ sound in them. Ask them to guess some of the foods that Shelly likes. If they guess a food correctly, make the puppet's mouth move while saying "m-m-m-m." If they guess a food that is incorrect, pretend Shelly spits it out. Remember to dignify incorrect responses by saying something like "Shelly would like that if she liked foods with the ____ sound in them," or "Maybe her friend Lolly the Lion would like that, but Shelly likes only those foods with the /sh/ sound in them."

   If the students cannot think of any foods that have the /sh/ sound, give them choices; for example, "Would Shelly like fish or bacon?" Another option is to tell them she likes all words with the /sh/ sound, which gives the students many more words to choose from. A third option would be to show two pictures: one of an item that contains /sh/, and another of an item that doesn't contain /sh/. The students choose the picture of the item that Shelly would like.

If a child gives the word *sugar* or another word that has the /sh/ sound but not the sound/spelling relationship, it is a correct response. Remember, you're looking for the /sh/ sound—not the letters.

2. Offer explicit instruction of the new sound/spelling relationship.

a. Hold up the letters *s* and *h* and tell the children that sometimes two letters make a special sound when they are put together. The two letters you are holding stand for the /sh/ sound. Show the children several pictures of things that are spelled with *sh*, such as *shark* and *dish*. Under each picture, display the word and have one child come up and circle, underline, or point to the *sh* in the word. Do this for all the pictures and words.

b. Then have the children call out other words they know with the *sh* letters or /sh/ sound in them. Start listing them in categories on the board or overhead projector. Possible categories are words that begin with *sh*, words that end with *sh*, words with *sh* in the middle, and words that have the /sh/ sound but not the letters *sh*.

3. Demonstrate blending of words and sentences. Engage the students in word-building exercises.

a. Show the students some words that have *sh* in them and blend the words, one at a time, using your favorite blending technique. Then write a sentence with one or more *sh* words. Read the sentence by blending the words that are decodable and spelling out the words that are irregular.

b. Then do a word-building activity. Give the students six or seven letters that they know, including *s* and *h*. Have them make two-letter words, then three-letter words, then four-letter words, and so on, using the letters you've given them. See the books *Making Words* and *Making More Words*, by Patricia Cunningham and Dorothy Hall (see page 158), for ideas. Then finish the activity by having the children put all the letters together to make one word. For example, if you give the children the letters *g, s, a, r, h, i,* and *n*, the word would be *sharing*.

4. Read a decodable or connected text where the sound/spelling relationship is frequently used.

a. Read the children a decodable book, one in which the phonics skill being taught is used frequently. (The *Wishy-Washy* books by Joy Cowley, from The Wright Group, are good examples.) You may wish to read one of these books to the children and have them bow every time they hear a word with the /sh/ sound in it.

b. If your basal series doesn't come with decodable books, or if you are unable to purchase any, make up a story with the children. Agree on four or five /sh/ words and then create a five- or six-sentence story using them.

5. Give children guided experiences in the dictation of words and sentences. Provide opportunities for them to write on their own.

    a. Dictate words with *sh* in them to the students. This is an opportunity to practice spelling *sh* words that are decodable. This is not a formal assessment, so feel free to guide the students so they all feel successful. End by dictating a sentence with some *sh* words and one or two irregular words. If the irregular words are on the word wall, it is OK to remind them of that.

    b. Give the students opportunities during center time or free time to create stories using /sh/ words. You may want to challenge them to write an alliteration. Add an element of fun by having them write a story where the other children have to guess how many /sh/ words there are without counting them.

For more samples of phonics lessons in this format, refer to the book *Phonics from A to Z: A Practical Guide*, by Wiley Blevins (see page 158).

We are always moving toward improvement,
not perfection. Do you celebrate the progress you
and your children make even though
it sometimes seems to happen in itty-bitty steps?
When was the last time you told yourself "Good Job!"?

PA/Phonics Activities

Sentence Team

SKILL:
Sentence segmentation

NUMBER OF STUDENTS:
Whole class, direct instruction

MATERIALS:
Sentences on sentence strips cut up into individual words; pocket chart; sentences below

DIRECTIONS:

1. Divide the class into groups of six.

2. Put the following sentences on sentence strips. Write each sentence several times (once for each group).

> I like to eat ice cream.
>
> A cat is under the chair.
>
> Please come to the soccer game.

3. Cut each sentence into separate words.

4. Put each cut-up sentence in an envelope. Give one envelope with the first cut-up sentence to each group.

5. Appoint a leader for each group. Have each leader distribute one word per student in the group.

6. Read the sentence out loud. Each group must stand shoulder-to-shoulder, with each student holding a word so the sentence is in the correct order.

7. Put the sentence on the pocket chart. Have each group check to see whether their sentence order is correct.

8. Ask the students to sit down. Each person should continue to hold his/her word.

9. Slowly call out each word of the sentence. When the student holding a word that you call out hears it, that student must stand up and then sit down.

10. Repeat the process with the second and third sentences.

Rhyme Time

SKILL:
Rhyme

NUMBER OF STUDENTS:
Whole class, direct instruction

MATERIALS:
Word cards (see words below)

DIRECTIONS:

1. Hold up a word card. Ask the class what the word is. Give the card to one child. Repeat the procedure until every child has a card.

2. Hold up a word, such as *sun*. All the children who are holding a word that rhymes with *sun* stand up and say "rhyme time." Each child standing reads the word on his/her card out loud, and the rest of the children indicate agreement or disagreement with a thumbs up or a thumbs down.

3. Suggested words for the teacher to use: had, bag, mat, net, did, top, hug, hot.

4. Suggested rhyming words for the children to use:

    dad, glad, mad, sad
    rag, tag, flag, wag
    cat, sat, fat, rat
    pet, set, met, bet
    rid, bid, lid, hid
    hop, mop, drop, stop
    rug, bug, mug, tug
    got, not, pot, spot

Find Your Partner

SKILL:
Syllable blending with compound words

NUMBER OF STUDENTS:
Whole class, direct instruction

MATERIALS:
Cards with compound word parts; pocket chart; high-energy cassette or CD, such as *Everybody Dance*, by Kimbo Educational, or *Kids Wanna Rock*, by Melody House

DIRECTIONS:

1. Distribute one card to each child.

2. Play high-energy music.

3. Children mingle with each other and search for the child holding the other part of their compound word.

4. When they find their partner, they put both their cards either in the pocket chart or on the chalk tray.

5. For children who find their partner early, they may assist the other children.

6. Compound words to be separated and put on cards:

sometime	inside
rainbow	football
cupcake	hotdog
doorbell	airplane
pancake	birdhouse
barnyard	bathrobe
without	milkshake

Syllable Search

SKILL:
Syllable counting

NUMBER OF STUDENTS:
Small group (4–6 students)

MATERIALS:
Spinner with three sections labeled 1, 2, and 3; chart paper; one book for each child, such as a trade book or library book

DIRECTIONS:

1. Distribute one book to each child.

2. Review one-, two-, and three-syllable words.

3. Spin the spinner. If it lands on 2, every child looks through his/her book, searching for two-syllable words.

4. Set up three columns on the chart paper, like the sample below. Put the students' words under the appropriate columns.

I'm Looking for a Word

SKILL:
Initial and final letters/sounds

NUMBER OF STUDENTS:
Small group (4–6 students)

MATERIALS:
Story on next page; window frames
(index cards with frames cut out; see reproducible
sample on next page)

DIRECTIONS:

1. Give each child a copy of the story *A Surprise for Mrs. Farkleface* (see next page).

2. Give each child a window frame.

3. Tell the children they are going on a word hunt and they have to find and frame the word that fits your description (see below). Once they find the word, they frame it with their window frame and raise their hand.

4. Here are some word-hunt suggestions:
I'm looking for a word in the first paragraph that begins with the same letter that starts the word *live*. (loved)

I'm looking for a word in the first paragraph that begins with the same letter that starts the word *get*. (grade, girls)

I'm looking for a word in the first paragraph that begins with the same letter that starts the word *sit* and makes the sound of /s/. (second, stop, school, say)

I'm looking for a word in the second paragraph that begins with the same sound that starts the word *choice*. (children)

I'm looking for a word in the second paragraph that ends with the same sound that ends the word *king*. (along)

I'm looking for a word in the second paragraph that ends with the same sound that ends the word *bat*. (fight, night)

5. Together, create an ending for the story. Decide on some beginning and ending sounds of words that must be included in the story.

VARIATION:

This game is suitable for use as a learning-center activity.

A Surprise for Mrs. Farkleface

Mrs. Farkleface loved her second-grade class. They were happy boys and girls, and they all loved school. She never had to stop the class and say, "Boys and girls, you are making too much noise," or "Boys and girls, please pay attention."

The children got along very well. They did not fight. They did not tease each other. They played very nicely together. She came home at night and told her family how lucky she was to have such a good class this year.

Then one day a very strange thing happened. Mrs. Farkleface was very surprised.

[Teacher and students create an ending for the story together.]

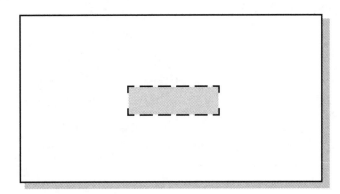

Look Around, I Have the Sound

SKILL:
Isolation of beginning sounds

NUMBER OF STUDENTS:
Small group (4–6 students)

MATERIALS:
Words on index cards (see word list below)

DIRECTIONS:

1. Give each child two cards, each with a different word on it. Ask each child to read his/her words and determine their beginning sounds.

2. Then say a word. If a child is holding a word that begins with the same sound as your word, the student stands up, holding the card, and says, "Look around, I have the sound." More than one person may end up standing at the same time.

3. Suggested words for the students to use:
met, rake, dip, pen, top, big, set, fan, nap, make, ran, door, pin, took, bat, sun, fat, net.

4. Suggested words for the teacher to use:
meat, read, duck, pot, tan, book, sand, farm, nice.

VARIATION:

Play the game using ending sounds instead of initial sounds.

Is the Sound the Same As...?

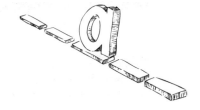

SKILLS:
Initial and final sounds; letter-sound correspondence

NUMBER OF STUDENTS:
Whole class, direct instruction

MATERIALS:
None

DIRECTIONS:

1. Choose a word. Put one line on the board for each letter in the word. Example: For the word *blast*, put five lines on the board. Fill in the vowel.

2. The students have to ask questions to guess the beginning sound first. The questions must be in this format: "Does it begin the same way as _____?" They must say a word that begins with the same sound and letter that they want to guess. For instance, if they want to guess the letter *b*, they might ask, "Does it begin the same way as *baby*?"

3. Once the students guess the first sound, they ask a question in the same format to guess the ending sound. For instance, if they want to guess the letter *p*, they might ask, "Does it end the same way as *map*?"

4. Once the first and last letters are guessed, students start the process with the second sound, and so forth.

5. Hint: Use only words that have a letter-sound correspondence. For instance, you could use *not*, but you could not use *knot*. Do not use words containing digraphs or silent letters.

6. Possible words to use: bat, tag, stop, red, skip, plug, tent, plant, drum, flag.

Hang 'Em Up

SKILL:
Blending onset and rime

NUMBER OF STUDENTS:
Whole class, direct instruction

MATERIALS:
Clothespins with consonants, consonant blends, and digraphs on them; large index cards with word families identical to the ones on the next page

DIRECTIONS:

1. In advance, tack up a clothesline with blank clothespins, attaching index cards with word families on them.

2. Divide the class into groups of four.

3. Distribute clothespins with consonants, consonant blends, and digraphs on them to each group.

> Group 1 gets clothespins that say *b*, *r*, *st*, and *s*.
> Group 2 gets clothespins that say *ch*, *l*, *bl*, and *f*.
> Group 3 gets clothespins that say *fl*, *r*, *c*, and *th*.
> Group 4 gets clothespins that say *sh*, *l*, *t*, and *h*.
> Group 5 gets clothespins that say *br*, *s*, *g*, and *r*.
> Group 6 gets clothespins that say *l*, *cl*, *p*, and *fr*.

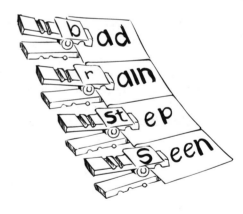

4. Take the cards down from the clothesline and give one to each group according to the group numbers indicated on the next page. Each group is to make new words by attaching their clothespins to the word families. Every clothespin needs to be used.

5. Check cards by reading the words to the entire class. Ask students to indicate agreement or disagreement with either a thumbs up or a thumbs down.

6. Hang up the cards. (See what the finished cards look like on the next page.)

b	ad		ch	op		fl	ip
r	ain		l	and		r	ug
st	ep		bl	ast		c	ook
s	een		f	an		th	em

Group One   Group Two   Group Three

sh	ip		br	ing		l	ine
l	og		s	et		cl	ock
t	en		g	ive		p	en
h	op		r	ag		fr	og

Group Four   Group Five   Group Six

Pass the Blend

SKILL:
Blending onset and rime

NUMBER OF STUDENTS:
Whole class, direct instruction

MATERIALS:
Consonant clusters and word families on index cards; noisemaker

DIRECTIONS:

1. Divide the students into groups of four. Have each group choose a designated "runner."

2. Give each group one consonant cluster and six word families.

3. Students make as many words as they can until they hear the buzzer. If they think they have made a legitimate word, they need to write it down. Allow about two minutes. Adjust the time as you think necessary.

4. Each "runner" then passes his/her group's consonant cluster to the group sitting to his/her group's right.

5. Each group tries to make words with the new cluster and their word families.

6. List of consonant clusters and word families:
Group 1: Start with *br* cluster. Word families include *ain, ee, ag, amp, um,* and *eam.*
Group 2: Start with *fr* cluster. Word families include *aid, esh, ake, op, ot,* and *ag.*
Group 3: Start with *fl* cluster. Word families include *ake, ail, ame, ory, ane,* and *um.*
Group 4: Start with *st* cluster. Word families include *ick, ame, ap, ain, ant,* and *op.*
Group 5: Start with *pl* cluster. Word families include *oom, ill, ay, age, ate,* and *ip.*
Group 6: Start with *dr* cluster. Word families include *ing, og, oat, ar, ace,* and *ain.*

5. When every group has had every cluster, the words are read and can be challenged by other groups. A dictionary settles the challenges.

Bingo or Challenge

SKILL:
Blending onset and rime

NUMBER OF STUDENTS:
Whole class, direct instruction

MATERIALS:
Word beginnings—one for each child (see list below)

DIRECTIONS:

1. Write a phonogram or word-family ending (i.e., rime) on the board (see list below).

2. Distribute a consonant, consonant cluster, or digraph to each student.

3. The students raise their hands if they think they are holding a card with a letter or letters that will make a real word when added to your rime.

4. Call on one student at a time to come up and put his/her card in front of your rime. He/she says the word. If the rest of the class agrees that it is a real word, they say "bingo." If not, they say "challenge."

5. Those who challenge must say why; for instance, "I don't think that is a real word." The original person must then use the word in a sentence.

6. The teacher then gives a "yay" or a "nay" or suggests using a dictionary.

7. Put a new rime on the board and continue the game.

8. Sample word beginnings to distribute to the children:
br, sh, ch, b, l, s, d, th, fl, st, f, g, h, m, n, p, r, t, w, bl, cl, tr, sn.

9. Sample word endings to put on the board:
ock, ag, en, an, ed, ing, ast, ip, ag, ap, ig, and, in, ame, ack.

Word Worms

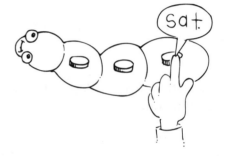

SKILLS:
Initial, medial, and final sounds; short vowels

NUMBER OF STUDENTS:
Whole class, direct instruction

MATERIALS:
Four counters per child; six word worms per child
(See reproducible on the next page; children may decorate their own word worms.)

DIRECTIONS:

1. Give each child a reproducible page of six word worms and four counters or manipulatives.

2. Tell the children to put their counters underneath the set of boxes in the first word worm—one per box.

3. Call out the word *sat*. Have them push up one counter per sound. Then, have them push the first counter above the first box and write in the letter *s*, push the second counter above the second box and write *a*, and so on.

4. Do the same with the following words: bed, flag, sit, rug, stop, drum.

Throw Me a Vowel

SKILLS:
Short vowel sounds; rhyming

NUMBER OF STUDENTS:
Small group (4–6 students)

MATERIALS:
Vowel beanbags (Take generic or homemade beanbags and tape a card with a vowel written on it to each one. You can even use masking tape with the vowel written on it in magic marker.)

DIRECTIONS:

1. Stand in a circle.

2. Throw out the beanbag that has an *a* on it to a student. That student thinks of a short-*a* word and says it out loud.

3. The student holding the beanbag throws it to another student, who must come up with a short-*a* word that rhymes with the first word.

4. That student says his/her rhyming short-*a* word out loud and then throws the beanbag to a new student, and so on.

5. After every student has had a turn, throw out a beanbag with a different vowel on it and start the process again.

Beat the Buzzer

SKILLS:
Phoneme blending; short vowels; spelling

NUMBER OF STUDENTS:
Whole class, direct instruction

MATERIALS:
Letters on large index cards; noisemaker

DIRECTIONS:

1. Call up five volunteers to the front of the room. Give them each a letter to hold.
(Put the vowels in a different color than the consonants.)

2. Call out a word.

3. The children at their seats repeat this chant:
    You can do it.
    Yes, you can.
    Build that word
    As fast as you can.

4. The children up at the front work together to make the word before you make the buzzer sound. You decide how long to give the team. (There are five children each holding a letter, but the words contain only three letters. The children have to work as a team to make the word.)

5. Once the word is made, the class decides whether it is correct.

6. Call up five new volunteers and repeat the process with a new set of letters.

7. Sample letters and words to use:

    c, k, a, n, m – can
    p, a, o, t, b – pot
    c, e, r, a, l – car
    e, m, n, t, d – met
    o, k, s, f, x – fox

Family Fun

SKILLS:
Phoneme blending; phoneme substitution

NUMBER OF STUDENTS:
Small group (4–6 students)

MATERIALS:
Word Family Board Game (see reproducible on page 126); Number Chart (see reproducibles on page 125); manila folder; one die; playing pieces

DIRECTIONS:

1. Glue a copy of the Word Family Board Game to one side of the manila folder. Glue a copy of the Number Chart to the other side. Laminate both sides.

2. Give each child a playing piece. You can use any manipulatives you want.

3. Tell the children that the numbers on the die will represent letters. Show them the list on the Number Chart.

4. Decide who goes first. That player rolls the die and moves the corresponding number of spaces on the board.

5. The player looks at the Number Chart to see what letter to use to put in front of the word family that his/her playing piece lands on. If the letter that the number on the die represents can be placed in front of the word family to make a real word, that player gets a point. If not, the player doesn't score.

6. The next player rolls the die and follows the same procedure.

7. All players must finish. The one with the most points at the end is the winner.

Note:

A player may challenge another player if he/she thinks the word is not a real word or is spelled wrong. A dictionary is then used to settle the challenge.

POTENTIAL WORDS

1 = r
rake, rat, run, rice, rate, ran, rack, rain

2 = b
bake, bat, bun, Ben, Bill, ban, back, bet

3 = f
fake, fat, fun, fate, fill, fan

4 = m
make, mat, mice, men, mate, mill, man, met, main

5 = p
pat, pun, pen, pill, pan, pack, pet, pain

6 = s
sake, sat, sun, sill, sack, set

Number Chart

1 = r

2 = b

3 = f

4 = m

5 = p

6 = s

Number Chart

1 = r

2 = b

3 = f

4 = m

5 = p

6 = s

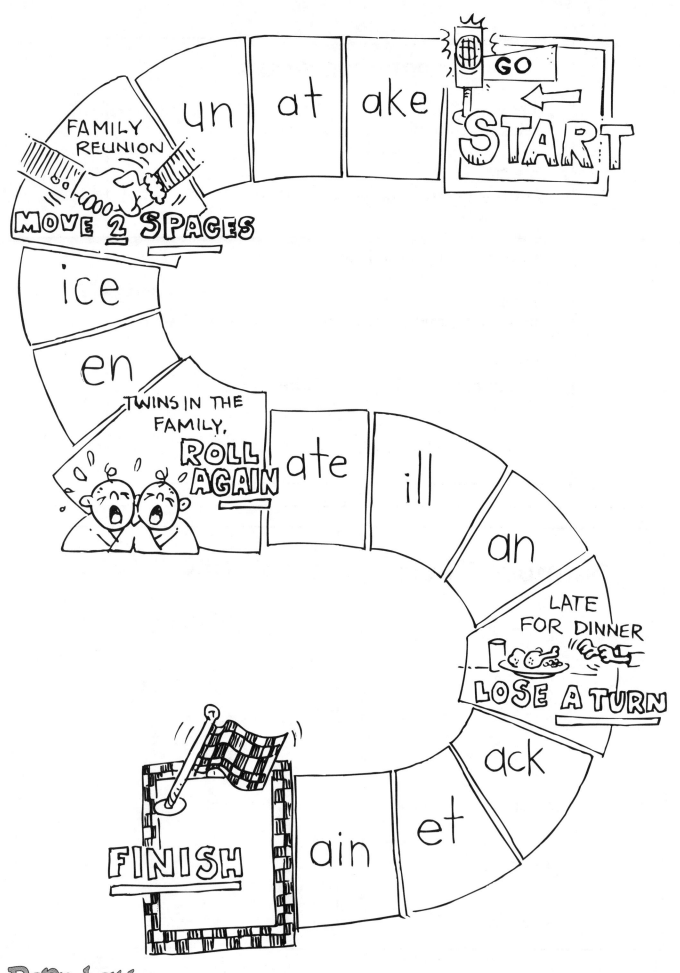

The Hungry Sound Monster

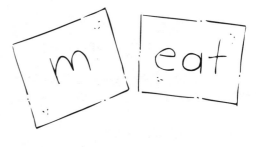

SKILL:
Phoneme deletion of initial sounds

NUMBER OF STUDENTS:
Whole class, direct instruction

MATERIALS:
Puppet to play the Hungry Sound Monster; words written on tagboard or index cards and cut into two pieces (One piece has the first letter on it, and the second piece has the rest of the word on it.)

DIRECTIONS:

1. Introduce the Hungry Sound Monster to the children. Use a puppet that you already have that has a mouth that opens and closes.

2. Tell them that the Hungry Sound Monster likes to eat the first sound in words.

3. Hold up a word, such as *meat*, and show it to the children. (Put the two pieces together.)

4. Ask the children what sound the Hungry Sound Monster would want to eat. The answer is /m/. Feed the /m/ to the Hungry Sound Monster.

5. Ask the children to tell you what part of the word is left: /eat/. Then hold it up.

6. Other suggested words to use: cat, block, bus, sent, trip, give, pan, cut.

Let's Say New Words

SKILL:
Substitution of final letter

NUMBER OF STUDENTS:
Whole class, direct instruction

MATERIALS:
Letter wraps (see illustration below)

DIRECTIONS:

1. Using the Elkonin box reproducible on page 75, make the letter wraps suggested in step 2 (see the sample below). Fold over each wrap on the last vertical line. When the wrap is folded over, the word on the wrap has the last letter missing. Add the new letter on the foldover, using a magic marker of a different color than the rest of the word.

2. Suggested words and new letters to use:
For *bag*, add *t*. For *hot*, add *p*. For *run*, add *b*. For *man*, add *d*. For *dig*, add *sh*. For *bell*, add *d*.

3. Sing this song to the tune of "Three Blind Mice":

   Let's say *bag*.
   Let's say *bag*.
   Remove the /g/ and put a /t/.
   And now the word is _____. (bat)

4. When singing the song, hold up the word wrap that says *bag*. When singing the line "Remove the /g/ and put a /t/," wrap the *t* around so the word spells *bat*.

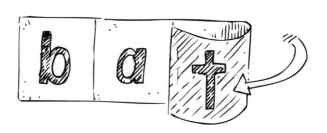

Watch My Family Grow

SKILL:
Phoneme substitution

NUMBER OF STUDENTS:
Whole class, direct instruction

MATERIALS:
Word-family sheet reproducible on next page

DIRECTIONS:

1. Have students choose partners. Give each pair a copy of the next page.

2. Tell the students that, for the first column, they are to make five words that end with *ot* and rhyme with *not*. For the second column, they are to make five words that end with *ake* and rhyme with *lake*. For the third column, they are to make five words that end with *an* and rhyme with *fan*. For the last column, they are to make five words that end with *ap* and rhyme with *cap*.

3. Students need to work in pairs. After a reasonable amount of time (which you determine), each pair passes their paper to the pair seated to their right. That pair determines if all the words on the paper are legitimate words. They may use a dictionary if they wish. If any words are challenged, the pair that does the challenging puts a C by the word(s) in question.

4. When the students are finished determining if the words are legitimate, the papers are given back to the original pairs. Each original pair must then write a sentence with any word that is being challenged.

5. The sentences are read to the whole class, where consensus must be reached about whether a word in question is real.

n**ot**

_____

_____

_____

_____

_____

lake

_____

_____

_____

_____

_____

f**an**

_____

_____

_____

_____

c**ap**

_____

_____

_____

_____

What's a Glif?

SKILL:
Decoding pseudowords

NUMBER OF STUDENTS:
Small group (4–6 students)

MATERIALS:
Container of pseudowords on index cards
(see list below)

DIRECTIONS:

1. Ask a student (the one whose last name comes first in the alphabet) to pick a card from the container of pseudowords. The student shows the word on the card to the rest of the class. He/she then attempts to pronounce it. The rest of the students indicate agreement or disagreement with the pronunciation with a thumbs up or a thumbs down.

2. If the student pronounces the word correctly, the student to his/her right attempts to say a word that rhymes with it. It can be a real word or a pseudoword.

3. If the student pronounces the word incorrectly, the student sitting to his/her right makes the next attempt.

4. Sample pseudowords to use for the container:

Consonant-Vowel-Consonant (CVC) Words

mal	leb	pud	vun
fot	pid	baf	deg

Vowel-Pattern Words

flove	zain	moy	jote
feen	dite	leat	foat

Consonant-Blend Words

bleb	frim	cret	brap
clon	stad	glif	flun

Can You Guess My Word?

SKILL:
Word-play activity (manipulating sounds and letters)

NUMBER OF STUDENTS:
Whole class, direct instruction

MATERIALS:
Magnetic letters and individual magnetic boards, or plain letters on students' desks; letters include *m, a, r, f, n,* and *e.*

DIRECTIONS:

1. Tell the students they are going to play a word-guessing game.

2. Give the students clues until they guess the word *farm.* For the first clue, say, "I'm thinking of a word that starts with *f.*"

3. Students manipulate their letters, trying to make a real word. After a reasonable amount of time passes, ask for some guesses.

4. If no one guesses the word, give the students another clue. The next one might be "There are two little words inside it." Repeat step 3.

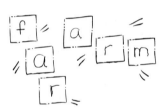

5. If the students don't guess the word, give them another clue. The next one might be "It rhymes with *harm.* What's the word?" At this point, the students should be able to guess the word *farm.*

6. Continue the game, using clues until the students guess the word *man.* Say, "I'm thinking of a word that begins with *m.*" If they don't guess the word, the next clue is "There is a little word inside it." The next clue is "It rhymes with *pan.*"

7. Once they guess *man,* tell the students to make two more words that rhyme with *man.*

8. Continue the "I'm thinking of a word" game with clues for such words as *men, mane, mare, fare, frame, ear,* and *near.*

Word Wall Prediction

SKILL:
Using the word wall

NUMBER OF STUDENTS:
Whole class, direct instruction

MATERIALS:
Pointer for each group

DIRECTIONS:

1. Divide the class into teams of four.

2. Tell the students you are thinking of a word on the word wall that has a silent letter. Members of each team put their heads together and agree on a word.

3. Call on a team. One of the members goes up to the word wall and points to the word the team thinks you have in mind. If it is correct, the student sits down, and you give a clue for the second word on your list. If it is not correct, give another clue for the word. A sample clue might be that the word has two vowels.

4. Repeat step 3.

5. Clues might include how many vowels, consonants, or syllables are in the word or what the word starts with, ends with, or rhymes with.

6. Sample words and clues to use:

ball
Clues:
    1. Has a little word inside it
    2. Has one vowel
    3. Begins the same as *baby*
    4. Has a double consonant
    5. Rhymes with *fall*

come
Clues:
    1. Has one syllable
    2. Has two vowels
    3. Has three sounds, or phonemes
    4. Has a silent letter
    5. Is the opposite of *go*

Sort Choices

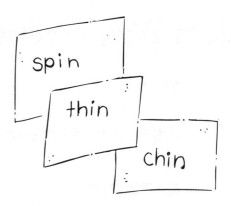

SKILL:
Word sorts

NUMBER OF STUDENTS:
Whole class, direct instruction

MATERIALS:
Words on index cards (six sets of 16 words)

DIRECTIONS:

1. Divide the class into groups of four.

2. Give each group a set of 16 words, one per index card. Each group gets the same words.

3. Tell the groups that they are to sort the words into categories of their choice ("open sorts").

4. Words to put on the index cards:

blue	black	chop	shine
spin	slip	chin	shore
from	glow	thin	thick
play	stop	chip	ship

5. Possible sort categories:
   Same initial sounds
   Same final sounds
   Same digraphs
   Same blends
   Same vowel sounds

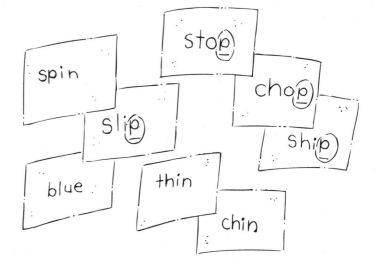

Do you think the activities in this book for phonological awareness and phonics are consistent with a brain-compatible environment? Choose one of the following responses.

A. No, learners learn best in a quiet environment with an absence of choice and fun. School should be highly structured, where the control-and-demand, stand-and-deliver model is valued.

B. Yes, the activities are fun and promote academic learning time where students understand the objective, are engaged and involved, and experience a 75 percent to 95 percent success rate. This contributes to a high-challenge, low-stress, brain-compatible learning environment.

C. No, there is too much interaction. A student's talking to others does not help the brain retain information. Students should be sitting in their chairs regurgitating the content when called on. After all, that is what I did in school, and I received excellent grades.

You chose A: No, learners learn best in a quiet environment with an absence of choice and fun. School should be highly structured, where the control-and-demand, stand-and-deliver model is valued.

Indeed, that was the model of choice for many, many years. The teacher controlled the information and was expected to "provide the learning" to the students. The teacher was the dispenser of golden nuggets of wisdom, and the students were the powerless containers. This old method, however, kept students from being accountable for their learning.

For students to be better able to retain information in their long-term memory, they need to participate in activities that relate to the objective, are meaningful, and involve many modalities, including movement and music. Students will enjoy the game-like activities in this book because they are fun and will cause their brains to produce and release natural opiates and endorphins. This helps the learner feel good and promotes optimal learning.

Was that really your final answer? You may want to go back and select another alternative more consistent with brain research.

You chose B: You are really using your brain! Yes, the activities are fun and promote academic learning time where students understand the objective, are engaged and involved, and experience a 75 percent to 95 percent success rate. This contributes to a high-challenge, low-stress, brain-compatible learning environment.

This answer best reflects the replicated research on the brain and its classroom implications. In *Begin with the Brain* (see page 159), Martha Kaufeldt says that humans are able to engage in optimal experiences in environments where there is a balance between challenge and low threat. Perceived threat and stress in the environment inhibit the brain and minimize its capabilities.

Students not meeting a success level when participating in activities will either act out or retreat. In either case, learning is not taking place. The multilevel activities in this book offer success to all children and opportunities for active participation and involvement.

You chose C: No, there is too much interaction. A student's talking to others does not help the brain retain information. Students should be sitting in their chairs regurgitating the content when called on. After all, that is what I did in school, and I received excellent grades.

Many of us, as students, played "the school game." We memorized our teachers' pearls of wisdom and repeated it verbatim on our tests. Some of us no longer remember those pearls because the experience wasn't meaningful or relevant to us. We didn't discuss the content or manipulate it.

In *Teaching with the Brain in Mind*, Eric Jensen says that there are two critical ingredients in any purposeful program to enrich the learner's brain. First, the learning must be challenging, presenting new information or experiences. Second, there must be some way to learn from the experience through interactive feedback.

In addition, in his book *Introduction to Brain-Compatible Learning*, Jensen says that the brain develops better in concert with others. Honoring that brain principle means creating learning environments that use teams, partners, and groups.

The PA activities suggested in this book are challenging and present new information and experiences; they frequently allow children to gather in groups or as partners; and they encourage feedback from other students.

Please go back and find a more brain-friendly alternative.

Practice doesn't make perfect; practice makes permanent.
If you practice something wrong again and again,
it will be permanently wrong. Are you patient with students
who have made continuous inappropriate choices
in the past, and do you explicitly teach them how to change
inappropriate problem-solving responses?

Parent Connection

Introduction

Research strongly indicates that parents and teachers working together enhances student achievement. Non-threatening ways to teach parents the skills they need to support your phonological awareness efforts with students include sending home parent letters with suggestions of engaging activities to do with their children, putting some of these ideas in a regular newsletter that goes home with the students, and sending home a parent calendar with more of these ideas. The following pages contain sample parent letters, which can assist you in accomplishing these goals.

Feel free to use this section as is, or integrate it into your existing parent programs. Since PA is a leading predictor of reading success, we must do all we can to encourage parents to be our allies in our efforts to help children become successful and fluent readers.

•   •   •

The first letter on page 142 describes a gathering where parents learn how to do a variety of PA activities with their children at home. You might ask parents to bring their children so they can do the activities together at the gathering.

The agenda for such a gathering could be as follows:

- Introduction of the facilitator(s) of the workshop.

- Discussion of what PA is and why our children need a PA foundation to be successful readers.

- Modeling of how to say some of the sounds of the letters, particularly *b, p, g, k, d, and t.*

- Introduction to the PA skills sequence.

- Demonstration of activities for each skill. (Choose activities from this book. If time allows, go through the answers to the calendar questions on page 147.)

- Question-and-answer period.

The facilitator(s) of the workshop might include teachers, reading specialists, speech pathologists, Title I personnel, Reading Recovery teachers, and so forth.

The meeting will be enhanced if you have refreshments available and if the main objective is to have fun together. An effective time window is between 60 and 90 minutes. Door prizes are always a nice additional incentive to get people to come.

Getting parents to come to workshops and gatherings is always a challenge for educators. Some of the following reality-based techniques are ones that I have used personally; others are ideas that teachers from around the country have shared with me. Consider using these suggestions to encourage parental attendance and to discourage the typical lament: "Why do we always have more teachers than parents attending a parent meeting?"

- Make sure the intent of the meeting is clear and that the parents' role is explained.
- Give parents ample notice in advance of the meeting.
- Provide transportation and child care, if possible.
- Keep the meeting brief, clear, and to the point.
- Allow parents to have input in the planning, if appropriate.
- Utilize community members as speakers.
- Consider having some meetings "off campus" in a more neutral area, such as a recreation center, church, synagogue, or training room in a mall.
- Combine the meeting with other school events or have students do a performance.
- Remember the three *f*'s: food, family, and fun.
- Consider serving a breakfast while a speaker gives a presentation.
- Send reminder notices home if the meeting involves a small number of parents.
- Offer multiple meetings/workshops at different times of the day (morning, afternoon, and evening) so more parents will be able to attend.
- Use a humorous food theme—doughnuts for Dad, muffins for Mom, goodies for grandparents.
- Provide videos for parents to borrow.
- Offer a Make and Take.
- Have the children make the invitations.

Dear Parent(s),

Experts in the field of reading have been telling us for a long time that good readers know how to recognize the sounds in words and manipulate, or play around, with these sounds. There are a number of sound skills that children need to know to become the best readers they can be. Some of them include the following:

• Recognizing individual words in sentences

• Rhyming

• Putting together, taking apart, and taking away parts of words

• Putting together, taking apart, and taking away individual sounds in words

You are invited to a parent gathering on [day of week], [date], at [time], where [name of person] will be sharing dozens of fun ideas and games parents can play with their children at home to strengthen these skills. Refreshments will be provided.

Don't miss this wonderful opportunity to find out how you can help your child be the best reader he/she can be. If you are able to participate, please fill out the information below and send it in with your child. Thank you.

[Name of teacher or principal]

– –

_____Yes, I will be able to attend the parent gathering on [date].

Name(s) of parent(s) and/or guests _____

Name of child _____

Name of child's teacher _____

Dear Parent(s),

Did you know that playing around with sounds can help your child be a better reader? When children know how to rhyme, identify beginning and ending sounds in words, and put together and take apart sounds in words, they will be better readers and spellers. Below are some games to play with your child to strengthen his/her rhyming skills. In the future, I will send home more letters with fun ways to help your child with other "playing with sounds" skills.

• Teach your child that words that sound alike at the end are rhyming words. Give your child examples, such as *cat*, *hat*, and *bat*. Tell your child to clap when you say two words that rhyme and to shake his/her head "no" when he/she hears two words that do not rhyme. Here are some suggested word pairs:

> go, so
>
> bag, run
>
> talk, walk
>
> hat, sun
>
> feet, hand
>
> sit, fit

• Tell your child you are going to play a game. Say three words and then ask him/her to figure out which word does not rhyme with the other two. Try these word sets:

> met, let, go
>
> came, run, name
>
> bat, bell, sell
>
> come, some, call

• Teach your child "Humpty Dumpty," "Hickory, Dickory, Dock," and "Jack Be Nimble." Ask him/her to figure out what the missing word is in these nursery rhymes.

> Humpty Dumpty sat on a wall.
>
> Humpty Dumpty had a great _____. (fall)

> Hickory, Dickory, Dock,
>
> The mouse ran up the _____. (clock)

> Jack be nimble, Jack be quick.
>
> Jack jump over the candle_____. (stick)

Dear Parent(s),

Today's letter will give you more ideas for helping your child play around with sounds in order to become a better reader. A very important skill that your child needs to master is the identification of beginning and ending sounds of words. Here are some fun ideas to help your child develop this critical pre-reading skill.

- Decide on a sound you want to help your child work on, such as /d/. (The slashes around the word serve as a reminder to say the sound of the letter, not the name of the letter.) Try not to say "duuuh." Keep the vowel sound after the /d/ as short as possible.

   • Talk about the /d/ sound with your child, and together look through magazines for pictures of items that begin with /d/. Have your child cut them out and paste them on a page dedicated to pictures of items that begin with /d/.

   • Every few days, make a new page of pictures of items beginning with a different sound. If your child is a more advanced reader, look for pictures of items that have that sound in the middle or the end of the word.

- Play picture-sort with your child, working on two different beginning sounds.

   • Cut out pictures from magazines or coloring books of items that begin with those sounds.

   • With your child, put the pictures in two rows. Put pictures of items beginning with one of the sounds in one row, and those of items beginning with the other sound in the second row. You might have a third row for pictures of items that do not begin with either sound.

- Help your child say the sounds /p/, /k/, and /t/. These should be said like a forced whisper and should be voiceless. A blast of air should come out of your child's mouth when he/she says those sounds. Have your child put a Kleenex in front of his/her mouth and see if it moves when he/she says those sounds. If it does, your child is probably saying the sounds correctly.

Dear Parent(s),

Today's letter will give you more ideas for helping your child play around with sounds in order to become a better reader. Another skill your child needs is to be able to separate, or segment, sounds of words, without thinking about the letters. Manipulating sounds will also help your child be a better speller. Here are some fun ideas for helping your child develop that important skill.

- Pause about a second after you say each sound in the word *bed*. Say "/b/ /e/ /d/." (The slashes around the letters are a reminder to say the sound of each letter, not the name of each letter.) Have your child hop as he/she says each sound in the word *bed*. Practice separating sounds in other words, such as *sit*, *hat*, *in*, and *fun*.

- Have fun practicing taking apart sounds of words, using cereal or checker pieces as counters. Put the counters in a straight line. Say a word, such as *big*. Have your child push up one counter while saying each sound—/b/ /i/ /g/. Do this with other words, such as *man*, *get*, *did*, and *sip*.

- Using the same words you used in the two activities above, have your child tap two pencils together for each of the sounds in the words.

- Say the following words normally. Then have your child stretch out each word, sound by sound. For example, say "bat." Your child should say "/b/ /a/ /t/." Other words to use include *lap*, *bit*, *go*, and *red*.

- Use the divided boxes on the following page for this activity. Give your child four counters that will fit inside the boxes. Put one under each box. Say a word, such as *hand*, and ask your child to push up a counter for each sound. A counter will fit into each box as your child says "/h/ /a/ /n/ /d/." Use words that have three or four sounds, such as *had*, *pen*, *fast*, *rat*, and *clap*. [Note to teachers: Make a copy of the reproducible Elkonin boxes on page 75 to enclose with each copy of this letter.]

Note: These games are played only with the sounds that make up words, not the letters.

JANUARY

2000

S	M	T	W	T	F	S
2	3 PLAY A WORD RIDDLE	4	5 HOW MANY WORDS END WITH /g/?	6	7 WHAT ARE THESE WORDS? ex /B/ /LACK/	8
9	10	11 HOW MANY WORDS RHYME WITH had?	12 CLAP THE WORDS IN THE SENTENCE	13	14	15
16	17 HOW MANY SOUNDS DO YOU HEAR?	18	19	20 HOW MANY PARTS IN YOUR NAME?	21 FIND 3 PICTURES THAT END WITH /r/	22
23	24	25 SAY A SILLY WORD THAT RHYMES	26 HOP THE # OF PARTS IN A WORD	27	28 GUESS A WORD	29
30	31					

Calendar Questions and Answers

Teachers: Consider sending home a calendar with a PA activity, question, or game for each day for a month (see sample at left). Here are some ideas:

1. Clap the words in the sentence "I like pizza." How many words are there?

2. Play a word riddle. Say, "I'm thinking of a word. It rhymes with *cat* and starts with a /b/."

3. Name as many words as you can think of that rhyme with *had*.

4. How many syllables, or parts, are there in the following words: *happy, elephant, rainbow, dog*?

5. Listen to this segmented word: /pic/ /nic/. Put the parts together and say the word.

6. How many words can you think of that start with /d/?

7. How many words can you think of that end with /g/?

8. Does *cat* rhyme with *sat*? Does *big* rhyme with *bag*? Does *sit* rhyme with *fit*?

9. Which word in this series does not rhyme with the others: *sun, run, rat*?

10. Finish this sentence: I walked out the door and went to the _____. Make your answer rhyme with the word *door*.

11. Say *football* without *foot*. Say *inside* without *side*. Say *louder* without *loud*.

12. How many sounds do you hear in these words: *fast, go, eat, pick*?

13. What are these words: /b/ /ack/, /d/ /ig/, /f/ /an/, /sh/ /eep/?

14. What are the last sounds you hear in these words: *beef, toad, pass, boat*?

15. How many syllables, or parts, in your name?

16. Take off the first sound in your name. How would you say your name now?

17. Take off the first sound in your name and add a /d/. What would it be?

18. Add a /t/ to /en/. What is the word? Add a /s/ to /top/. What is the word?

19. Find three pictures of things that begin with /r/.

20. Say "fan." Say it again, but don't say /f/. Say "boy." Say it again, but don't say /b/.

21. Say "hat." Change the /h/ to /m/. What's the word? Say "pick." Change the /p/ to /s/. What is the word?

22. Say a silly word that rhymes with *big*. Say a silly word that rhymes with *apple*.

23. Cut out pictures of three things that end with /k/.

24. Draw a picture of two things that begin with the same sound that begins your name.

25. Hop the number of parts, or syllables, in each of these words: *happy, baseball, umbrella, eat*.

26. At dinner tonight, find something on the table that begins with /s/.

27. Guess this word: It has two parts, or syllables. It begins with /w/. It is something that you drink.

28. If I say "/be/ /cause/," you say "because." If I say "/din/ /ner/," you say _____. If I say "/mon/ /ster/," you say _____.

29. What are the first sounds that you hear in these words: *kitten, get, top, big, rope, last*? (Let the child give an answer after each word.)

30. What are the last sounds that you hear in these words: *tap, right, see, table*?

31. Roll one die. Think of a word that rhymes with the number you rolled. Roll and rhyme three more times.

Possible Answers to Calendar Questions

1. 3

2. bat

3. Possible words include *bad, dad, fad, had, lad, mad, pad, sad,* etc. It's OK if the child comes up with a silly word, such as *jad* or *zad*.

4. 2, 3, 2, 1

5. picnic

6. Any real words, such as *dish, day, door,* etc., or silly words, such as *dof, diffle, dake,* etc., are OK.

7. Possible words include *bag, pig, leg, flag,* etc.

8. yes, no, yes

9. rat

10. *store,* or any other rhyming word that would make sense

11. ball, in, er

12. 4, 2, 2, 3

13. back, dig, fan, sheep

14. /f/, /d/, /s/, /t/

15. Help your child figure it out by clapping the parts.

16. Examples: *Linda* would be *inda, Chad* would be *ad,* and *Willie* would be *illie.*

17. Examples: *Marie* would be *Darie, Paul* would be *Daul,* and *Jenny* would be *Denny.*

18. ten, stop

19. Examples might be a picture of a rabbit, ring, rock, etc.

20. an, oy

21. mat, sick

22. Examples of silly words that rhyme with *big* could be *tig, lig,* etc. Examples of silly words that rhyme with *apple* could be *bapple, fapple,* etc.

23. Examples might be a picture of a block, cake, sink, etc.

24. If your child's name is Chad or Shelly, remember that /ch/ is one sound and /sh/ is one sound.

25. 2 hops, 2 hops, 3 hops, 1 hop

26. Examples might be salad, silverware, or soup.

27. water

28. dinner, monster

29. /k/, /g/, /t/, /b/, /r/, /l/

30. /p/, /t/, /e/, /l/

31. Examples might be: one – sun, two – shoe, three – tree, four – door, five – hive, six – sticks.

More Ideas for Parents

Consider a parent corner for your newsletter that includes ideas for PA activities parents can do with their children. Parents are more likely to read activities if they are short and include graphics. Here are some suggestions.

- Help your child learn the love of reading. Arrange for a quiet time at least four times a week where your child reads for 10 to 20 minutes.

- Play rhyming games with your child. Say a nursery rhyme and leave out the rhyming word. Let your child say the missing word. Example: Mary had a little lamb; its fleece was white as snow. Everywhere that Mary went, her lamb was sure to _____.

- Play a syllable-clapping game with your child. Name some common objects around the house and have your child clap the number of syllables. For example: *pencil* (two claps), *toothbrush* (two claps), *television* (four claps).

- Tell your child that you are going to play a pretending game. You will pretend you are an old, old, old storyteller. It takes you a long time to say words; you are going to say them in a strange way. See if your child can guess the word after you say each one. Allow about a second between syllables. Suggested words to use: cow – boy, play – ground, fun – ny, lit – tle, win – ter, in – to.

- Ask your child to tell you his/her favorite foods. After your child names each food, ask him/her what sound it begins with. Remember, you're looking for sounds, not letters.

- Have your child figure out the rhyming words to put in the blanks below.

  Crazy Rhymin' Simon says "Touch your *shed*." He means "Touch your head."
  Rhymin' Simon says "Touch your *belbow*." He means "Touch your _____."
  Rhymin' Simon says "Touch your *jummy*." He means "Touch your _____."
  Rhymin' Simon says "Touch your *doze*." He means "Touch your _____."

- Talk about words and their sounds when you go grocery shopping. When buying fruit, ask your child what sounds are alike in these two names of fruits: pears and pineapple.

- Play with sounds by making up silly songs. Add new sounds to the beginning of words in popular songs. For example, instead of "Happy birthday to you," sing "Babby birthday boo boo." Try different songs, and begin the words with the sound that begins your child's name.

- Put some common items you have around the house together in a bag. Let your child pick out an object from the bag. Name the object and then ask your child to think of a real word or a silly word that rhymes with the name of that object. Example: If your child picks a rag out of the bag, your child may say a real rhyming word, such as *tag*, or a silly rhyming word, such as *dag*. Any word is OK as long as it rhymes.

Parents are children's first reading teachers. Promoting literacy at home through reading to children, modeling that reading is important, and visiting the library are common activities schools encourage parents to do with their children.

Which of the following three ideas would be appropriate for inclusion in a school newsletter that promotes literacy at home? (Note: This question is for the readers of this book who are interested in parental involvement. This is not a parent handout.)

A. Read to your child after school, after dinner, and two hours before bedtime. The more you read to your child, the better reader your child will become.

B. Make your home like a school when your child comes home. Find out what the teacher's plans and objectives were and review the entire day with your child. Make sure you include a pop quiz at the end.

C. Find teachable moments in your daily activities to help your child learn and be excited about the sounds of our language. Examples might include the following:

- While driving to the store with your child, ask him/her to tell you the first sound in the name of the store.
- While baking cookies with your child, tell him/her that the Cookie Monster has trouble rhyming words. Ask your child to help by telling you words that rhyme with various words you read from the recipe.
- Tell your child to clap the number of syllables, or parts, in the names of everyone in your family.

You chose A: Read to your child after school, after dinner, and two hours before bedtime. The more you read to your child, the better reader your child will become.

Although reading at home to children is very important and should not be minimized, reading continually can turn a child off to the idea of reading and increase behavioral problems. In addition, reading nonstop does not honor a child's developmental stages.

Parents' reading a story a day to children is admirable. In addition, children should be reading independently at least four nights a week. Young children who are emergent readers can "read the pictures" for five to seven minutes. Children who are more proficient readers need to read from 10 minutes a night in first grade to 20 minutes a night in second grade.

Please go back and select another alternative for your school newsletter.

You chose B: Make your home like a school when your child comes home. Find out what the teacher's plans and objectives were and review the entire day with your child. Make sure you include a pop quiz at the end.

Promoting literacy at home does not mean establishing a simulated school setting, reteaching the material, and testing a child. Children need time to play and relax. Overemphasizing school can turn students off to the idea of school and may even cause hostility and rebellion.

Finding a balance of teachable moments at home, sharing the day, reinforcing skills, and building in homework time are challenges for parents. Teachers are often frustrated with parents who provide little or no support at home. However, spending too much time creating a school atmosphere can be discouraging for children.

Please go back and select another alternative for your newsletter that will promote a parent/teacher partnership in literacy.

You chose C: Find teachable moments in your daily activities to help your child be excited about letters, words, and language.

Either you are a parent yourself or you have a good handle on parental involvement. This is the correct answer.

Teachable moments are excellent ways to stimulate excitement and motivation about learning. These moments are meaningful and relevant to children, and therefore they are more likely to be remembered. They can also be a nice opportunity for parents and children to spend some special, quality time together.

Indexes, Glossary, & Resources

Index of Phonological Awareness Activities

Index of Phonological Awareness & Phonics Activities

Glossary

Brain-compatible strategies—Strategies used in the classroom that are compatible with the way in which the brain optimally learns.

Consonant blends—Two or more consonants together that maintain their own sounds when spoken; for example, /cl/ in *clap*, /spr/ in *spring*.

Consonant cluster—The written form of a consonant blend.

Continuant sounds—Sounds that you can say or stretch as long as you have air in your lungs; for example, /s/, /l/, and /m/.

Decoding—The ability to translate letters to sounds, syllables, and words.

Digraph—Two letters together that represent one sound; for example, /sh/, /ch/, /th/, and /wh/.

Diphthong—Vowel sounds formed by a gliding action in the mouth; for example, /ou/ in *house*, /oy/ in *boy*.

Onset—The consonant or consonant blend at the beginning of a syllable; the remainder of the syllable is called *rime*. In *stop*, /st/ is the onset and /op/ is the rime.

PAST—Phonological Awareness Skills Test, an assessment that tests students on the PA skills sequence.

Phoneme—The individual units of sound in a word. For example, in the word *hand*, there are four phonemes: /h/, /a/, /n/, and /d/.

Phonemic awareness—The ability to manipulate the individual units of sounds in words; for example, recognizing initial, medial, and final sounds of words; blending, segmenting, and deleting sounds; and manipulating sounds. It fits under the phonological awareness skills sequence.

Phonics—Recognizing the letter-sound correspondence in words; phonics and phonological awareness are inextricably woven.

Phonological awareness—Understanding the structure of our words and how they are broken down; it involves the ability to notice and manipulate the sounds in words. Abbreviated as *PA*.

Phonological awareness skills sequence—Includes concept of spoken word; rhyme; syllables; phonemes; and phoneme manipulation.

Plosive sounds—These sounds are formed by blocking off the air flow and then letting out a puff of air, such as in /b/, /p/, /g/, /k/, /d/, and /t.

Pseudowords—Words that are not real but are decodable; for example, *gup*, *ral*, and *sif*.

Rhyming words—Words that sound the same at the end; for example, *mat*, *cat*, and *rat*.

Rime—The vowel and all the letters that follow it in a syllable; is preceded by an *onset*, or consonant(s) at the beginning of the syllable. For example, /at/ in *cat*, /eep/ in *sheep*.

Stop sounds—Sounds that you cannot say continuously, such as /g/, /j/, /w/, and /y/.

Syllable—A unit of spoken language; contains a vowel or vowel sound.

Word sort—Categorizing words by a certain criterion; for example, sorting words by initial sound, final sound, or vowel pattern.

Word wall—A wall on which words are displayed under the alphabet; usually contains irregular or high-frequency words. For example, under *H* you might have the words *have*, *here*, and *house*.

Suggested Reading

Adams, Marilyn Jager, Barbara R. Foorman, Ingvar Lundberg, and Terri Beeler. *Phonemic Awareness in Young Children*. Baltimore, MD: Paul H. Brookes Publishing Co., 1998.

Albert, Linda. *Cooperative Discipline*. Circle Pines, MN: American Guidance Service, Inc., 1996.

Allington, Richard L., and Patricia M. Cunningham. *Schools That Work: Where All Children Read and Write*. Reading, MA: Addison-Wesley Publishing Co., 1995.

Bear, Donald R., Marcia Invernizzi, Shane Templeton, and Francine Johnston. *Words Their Way*, 2d ed. Upper Saddle River, NJ: Prentice-Hall, Inc., 2000.

Blevins, Wiley. *Phonemic Awareness Activities for Early Reading Success*. New York: Scholastic Professional Books, 1997.

_____. *Phonics from A to Z: A Practical Guide*. New York: Scholastic Professional Books, 1998.

Cunningham, Patricia M. *Phonics They Use: Words for Reading and Writing*, 3d ed. New York: Addison-Wesley Educational Publishers Inc., 2000.

Cunningham, Patricia M., and Richard L. Allington. *Classrooms That Work: They Can All Read and Write*. New York: HarperCollins College Publishers, 1994.

Cunningham, Patricia M., and Dorothy P. Hall. *Making Big Words*. Torrance, CA: Good Apple, 1994. (*Making More Big Words*, by the same authors, is also available. Both books are for grades 3–6.)

_____. *Making Words*. Torrance, CA: Good Apple, 1994. (*Making More Words*, by the same authors, is also available. Both books are for grades 1–3.)

_____. *Month-by-Month Phonics*. Greensboro, NC: Carson-Dellosa Publishing Company, Inc., 1997. (This series includes a book for each grade from K–3, and one for upper grades.)

Cunningham, Patricia M., Dorothy P. Hall, and Cheryl M. Sigmon. *The Teacher's Guide to the Four Blocks: A Multimethod, Multilevel Framework for Grades 1–3*. Greensboro, NC: Carson-Dellosa Publishing Company, Inc., 1999.

Fitzpatrick, Jo. *Phonemic Awareness: Playing with Sounds to Strengthen Beginning Reading Skills*. Cypress, CA: Creative Teaching Press, Inc., 1997.

_____. *Reading Strategies That Work: Helping Young Readers Develop Independent Reading Skills*. Cypress, CA: Creative Teaching Press, Inc., 1998.

Fountas, Irene C., and Gay Su Pinnell. *Guided Reading*. Portsmouth, NH: Heinemann, 1996.

_____. *Matching Books to Readers: Using Leveled Books in Guided Reading, K–3*. Portsmouth, NH: Heinemann, 1999.

Fry, Edward Bernard, Jacqueline E. Kress, and Dona Lee Fountoukidis. *The Reading Teacher's Book of Lists*. West Nyack, NY: The Center for Applied Research in Education, 1993.

Goldsworthy, Candance L. *Sourcebook of Phonological Awareness Activities: Children's Classic Literature*. San Diego, CA: Singular Publishing Group, Inc., 1998.

Healy, Jane M. *Endangered Minds: Why Children Don't Think and What We Can Do About It*. New York: Simon & Schuster, 1990.

_____. *Your Child's Growing Mind*. Revised and updated edition. New York: Doubleday, 1994.

Holliman, Linda. *The Complete Guide to Classroom Centers*. Cypress, CA: Creative Teaching Press, Inc., 1996.

Hoyt, Linda. *Revisit, Reflect, Retell: Strategies for Improving Reading Comprehension*. Portsmouth, NH: Heinemann, 1999.

Ingraham, Phoebe Bell. *Creating & Managing Learning Centers: A Thematic Approach*. Peterborough, NH: Crystal Springs Books, 1997.

Jensen, Eric. *Introduction to Brain-Compatible Learning*. San Diego, CA: The Brain Store, Inc., 1998.

_____. *Super Teaching*, 3rd ed. San Diego, CA: The Brain Store, Inc., 1995.

_____. *Teaching with the Brain in Mind*. Alexandria, VA: ASCD, 1998.

Jordano, Kimberly, and Trisha Callella-Jones. *Phonemic Awareness Songs & Rhymes*. Cypress, CA: Creative Teaching Press, Inc., 1998. (This series includes three books: one each for winter, spring, and fall.)

Kaufeldt, Martha. *Begin with the Brain: Orchestrating the Learner-Centered Classroom*. Tucson, AZ: Zephyr Press, 1999.

Marriott, Donna. *What Are the Other Kids Doing While You Teach Small Groups?* Cypress, CA: Creative Teaching Press, Inc., 1997.

McCarrier, Andrea, Gay Su Pinnell, and Irene C. Fountas. *Interactive Writing*. Portsmouth, NH: Heinemann, 2000.

Pavelka, Patricia. *Create Independent Learners: Teacher-Tested Strategies for All Ability Levels*. Peterborough, NH: Crystal Springs Books, 1999.

_____. *Making the Connection: Learning Skills Through Literature*. Peterborough, NH: Crystal Springs Books, 1995, 1997. (K–2 and 3–6 versions are available.)

Payne, Ruby K. *A Framework for Understanding Poverty*. Baytown, TX: RFT Publishing Co., 1998.

Pinnell, Gay Su, and Irene C. Fountas. *Word Matters*. Portsmouth, NH: Heinemann, 1998.

Snow, Catherine, M. Susan Burns, and Peg Griffin, eds. *Preventing Reading Difficulties in Young Children*. Washington, DC: National Academy Press, 1999.

_____. *Starting Out Right: A Guide to Promoting Children's Reading Success*. Washington, DC: National Academy Press, 1999.

Recommended Web Sites

Literacy Web Sites—All Grade Levels

www.reading.org
International Reading Association

Listserv@listserv.syr.edu
International Reading Association—subscribe to an on-line global discussion group

http://darkwing.uoregon.edu/~ncite/read.html
Helping Children with Learning Disabilities

http://teams.lacoe.edu/documentation/places/language.html
L.A. County Office of Education—reading and writing links

www.teachernet.com

Literacy Web Sites—Primary Grades

www.wfu.edu/~cunningh/fourblocks/
The Four Blocks Classroom Plan, by Pat Cunningham and Dorothy Hall

www.geocities.com/Heartland/hollow/1213/centers
Ideas for literacy centers

http://www.geocities.com/Wellesley/Atrium/1783/Centers.html
Many research-based activities for phonological awareness, centers, literature circles, guided reading, etc.

General

For a comprehensive list of more great Web sites for educators, see
www.mainecenter.org/seed/sites.